I've written this book for my daughters,
and every man's daughters. . . .

Every man knows there are secrets we discuss among the boys that we would never discuss with women, but our daughters are the ones who need that knowledge the most. I want to make sure my daughters retain everything I have to share with them, so in addition to the lifetime of lessons they will learn from our conversations and the example I provide, they will also have the benefit of having it in the form of a book.

When I started to write this book, I realized there are many women who could benefit from the secrets I am imparting. The lessons here are invaluable, and it doesn't matter who you are or how old you are; every lady on earth is someone's daughter. I invite you to join me as I teach my daughters the lessons your fathers would have wanted you to know.

—Michael Lockwood

WOMEN HAVE ALL THE POWER

Too Bad They Don't Know It!

MICHAEL J. LOCKWOOD

BERKLEY BOOKS, NEW YORK

THE BERKLEY PUBLISHING GROUP
Published by the Penguin Group
Penguin Group (USA) Inc.
375 Hudson Street, New York, New York 10014, USA
Penguin Group (Canada), 90 Eglinton Avenue East, Suite 700, Toronto, Ontario M4P 2Y3, Canada
(a division of Pearson Penguin Canada Inc.)
Penguin Books Ltd., 80 Strand, London WC2R 0RL, England
Penguin Group Ireland, 25 St. Stephen's Green, Dublin 2, Ireland (a division of Penguin Books Ltd.)
Penguin Group (Australia), 250 Camberwell Road, Camberwell, Victoria 3124, Australia
(a division of Pearson Australia Group Pty. Ltd.)
Penguin Books India Pvt. Ltd., 11 Community Centre, Panchsheel Park, New Delhi—110 017, India
Penguin Group (NZ), 67 Apollo Drive, Rosedale, North Shore, 0632, New Zealand
(a division of Pearson New Zealand Ltd.)
Penguin Books (South Africa) (Pty.) Ltd., 24 Sturdee Avenue, Rosebank, Johannesburg 2196,
South Africa

Penguin Books Ltd., Registered Offices: 80 Strand, London WC2R 0RL, England

Cover design by Rita Frangie
Cover art by S. Miroque
Book design by Kristin del Rosario

PRINTING HISTORY
L. L. Publishing Company edition / 2008
Berkley trade paperback edition / August 2010

Berkley trade paperback ISBN: 978-0-425-23451-8

Library of Congress Cataloging-in-Publication Data

Lockwood, Michael J.
Women have all the power— : too bad they don't know it! : secrets every man's daughter should know / Michael J. Lockwood. — 1st ed.
p. cm.
Originally published: Cedar Hill, TX : L. L. Pub. Co., c2008.
ISBN 978-0-425-23451-8 (alk. paper)
1. Man-woman relationships. 2. Dating (Social customs) 3. Mate selection. 4. Women—Psychology. 5. Men—Psychology. I. Title.
HQ801.L5886 2010
305.3—dc22

2010012306

PRINTED IN THE UNITED STATES OF AMERICA

10 9 8 7 6 5

This book is dedicated to my three daughters, Gabrielle, Mikaela, and Lauren. Use it wisely. May God bless, guide, and protect you all the days of your lives.

—Dad

ACKNOWLEDGMENTS

First and foremost, I owe all the praise and glory to God, who inspired me to take on this endeavor. I also thank God for allowing me to experience all of the joyous and painful moments that have contributed to my growth in relationships. Only now do I understand the reason: I was used as an instrument to make the path a little smoother for those who come after me. My maturity has enabled me to be a better husband, a better father, and a better man in general.

I'd like to thank my parents, Pam, Don, and Joe, for the examples that they've set. Mom, you've been a pillar of strength. You often made a way out of no way. Regardless of how much we had or didn't have, you always found a way to make our house a home. Though you have worked as long as I can remember, you never compromised your position as a mother and a wife. Dad, you made me a man. Without you as an example, there's no telling where I would have ended up. You guided me through adolescence, which set the standard for the rest of my life. Your contribution to my development has been invaluable. Dad, I thank you for being there in adulthood. You've been a friend and someone I could always talk to when I needed someone to trust. Thank you all for your sacrifices.

To my beautiful daughters, Gabrielle and Mikaela, you have always been the best children any man could possibly desire. You've both been obedient and disciplined throughout your childhood. You're wonderful students and classy young ladies. Continue to make your daddy proud by carrying yourselves with dignity and grace. I pray that God continues to bless and guide you. This book is dedicated to you.

Lauren, daughter number three, although you are only three years old, I can pretty much predict how you will be as an adult. Besides being incredibly beautiful and smart, I know that you will be an independent thinker. You always march to your own beat, and one of your favorite phrases is, "Daddy, I want to do all by myself." You will also be all of the challenge that a man can dream of, because you are one feisty little girl. By the time you're able to read and understand this book, I pray women will have taken their rightful position. If not, take your proper role by internalizing these timeless words.

MJ, my only son, it took me eighteen years to figure out how to get you here, but it was well worth the wait. I plan on spending the rest of my days mentoring, teaching, and raising you to be a man of virtue and valor. I'm counting on you to carry the family name with great honor. I love you.

Dawn, never settle. There's a man out there for you, and I look forward to the day you choose your husband. I believe I'm due for some nieces and nephews.

Tony, I'm still waiting for you to break the shackles and claim the life you're due.

In loving memory of my second mother, Betty. Rest in peace.

I chose to save the last words for my wife, Lisa, the love of my life. You are the virtuous one I've always dreamed of. Thank you for your patience and support as I completed the work with which God has tasked me. You represent everything that is good about marriage and the divine bond intended for a man and a woman. Thank you for being the woman you are. I look forward to spending the rest of my life with you.

CONTENTS

FOREWORD BY VIVICA A. FOX XIII

INTRODUCTION XV

1. Aren't You Tired? 1
2. Man-Ology 25
3. Stay in Your Own Lane 71
4. Keeping the "Piece" 113
5. Give Him a "Peace" 151
6. The New School Woman 179
7. No War and "Piece" 213
8. Power Reclaimed 239

APPENDIX 245

FOREWORD

by Vivica A. Fox

For so long we have placed the blame on men when relationships have gone wrong. Granted, they carry their share of the burden, but it's time for a reality check. If we, as women, collectively start to set our expectations higher and examine what we're willing to accept from men, they will find a way to meet our demands. We've allowed them to run game and have lowered our standards to meet their needs while sacrificing our own. That's why it is so difficult to find a good man who is willing to commit, be a good husband, and take care of his children. We let them get away with this nonsense.

It's common knowledge that I've been married, divorced, and had a very public breakup, but I'm still standing strong. Michael Lockwood has given us all a wake-up call. This book has given me encouragement, an insightful perspective on men, and a renewed sense of purpose. Girlfriends, this is a man who is tactfully telling us what we should have been able to figure out well before now.

One of my favorite quotes from the book is "A man convinced against his will is of the same opinion still." It's profound, yet so true. When we find a man, we tend to try to mold him into what we want him to be instead of accepting him for who he is. Michael makes it clear that all the molding in the world won't change him if he doesn't want to be changed.

The lessons here are life altering and long overdue. If you're willing to accept the challenges Michael puts forth, it will not only change the way you view dating and marriage, it will impart in you a greater sense of pride and purpose. With so many of our children being raised without a father in the home, it's refreshing to have a daddy who is willing to share the secrets men tend to keep to themselves.

The title says it all. We do have all the power, and now we know it as well.

INTRODUCTION

Gabrielle, Mikaela, and Lauren:

Girls, as I write this, you are still children, but I am moved to commit to paper the lessons I am compelled to teach you. From the first moment I laid eyes on you, I finally realized the mighty love a parent has for a child. Yes, I had been the fortunate recipient of that kind of love; your grandparents were everything parents are supposed to be. But it was only when I became a parent myself, when the nurse gently placed you in my arms, that I fully comprehended the magnitude of parental love. There was adoration, unconditional love, and a fierce desire to always protect you from harm. So I have made it my responsibility to impart to you certain truths.

If you were to read this today, you might not understand some of the language I use here nor fully comprehend all of the information that I am sharing. However, I know that when the time is right, you will have a written resource to turn to. Some of the language I have chosen to use may seem blunt. This isn't to shock you, but who would profit if I tiptoed around the issues using only niceties? I choose to use language that some may consider harsh, but life itself can be very harsh, and the truth also is often very harsh. Candy-coating things tends to devalue their importance, and I have some very important lessons that can only be completely understood if I am completely honest and candid. So while you may not fully comprehend everything I say here, the fundamental message is vital for girls and women of all ages. Until you are old enough to understand these words, I hope I share the essence of these lessons through my actions and my interactions with you. Your father adores you.

This book is ultimately about men and interacting with them. It is very, very important that I explain this aspect of life. Not being able to handle yourself and your self-image as it relates to men can be devastating. Making bad decisions when it comes to relationships can completely and thoroughly ruin your life. It can ruin your self-esteem, your educational prospects, and your family life, both present and future. It can literally smother your dreams. Picking the wrong man can be a death sentence. I want you to take this book, read it, reference it from time to time, and it will save you a whole lot of heartache. Now, don't be selfish with it either. I'm sure you know a few of your friends who need a copy of their own, and when you have children, you should ensure that they too have the opportunity to learn these same valuable lessons. As you go through life you will come across many women who have destructive habits when dealing with men. That's when the words of this book will ring loudest in your head, and I hope you thank God you had a father who loved you so much that he made sure you didn't fall victim to self-sabotage and the methods that men sometimes use to undermine your value.

As a father, my job is to set the standard for the men you choose to have in your life. Although I am definitely not perfect and have experienced my share of life's ups and downs, it's important for me to always be a positive example for you. After all, everyone can deal with the good things in life, but it's how you deal with the challenges that sets you apart. Always remember, I would never disrespect you, and you should never be with a man who disrespects you. I don't call you out of your name, and you should never settle for a man who does. I don't physically abuse you, and you better not *ever* let a man put his hands on you in violence. The best way for you to learn how to recognize a good man is for me to be one. I set the standard. I remember the face you gave me when I told you I wanted to take you out on a date. You didn't understand at the time, but I understood all along. My intent was to demonstrate how you were supposed to be treated while on a date, instead of preaching it. Who could possibly be a better example of a good date than your own father?

I remember honking the car horn to see if you would

come to the car, only to make you go back in the house and wait for me to come and ring the doorbell to get you. I made sure that I opened the car door for you, so you didn't feel that it was normal for a young lady to open the door on her own. How about the time that we went out to dinner and I pushed the check to you in an attempt to see if you would pay? You acted as if you didn't even see my gesture. I was happy to see that you were progressing quite well. I still smile to myself when I think about the time that I pulled out your chair for you. The look on your face was like, "Why do I want him to pull out my chair when I end up sitting two feet from where I'm supposed to?" That was only until I taught you to gracefully rise up so I could slide you and your chair to the proper distance. What great memories. Remember them on every date you go on and never settle for less.

A father is supposed to protect you and keep you under his wing until you are ready to fly. However, I can't and won't keep you so protected and sheltered that you are unable to function in the world. The world can be very cruel. As you turn through the pages of this book, you'll learn some of the good, the bad, and the ugly the world has to offer. I just need you to trust that what I'm saying is true. Trust that the things I'm going to teach you are for your own good. I taught you how to swim, right? You trusted me and never drowned. I taught you how to roller-skate, right? You trusted I would not let you fall. I taught you how to ride a bike, right? You may have gotten a couple of bumps and bruises along the way, but the important part to remember is that now you are wonderful swimmers, great skaters, and incredible bicyclists. So, what would ever make you stop trusting me now? Hopefully nothing. My job is to teach you the ways of the world so you can tackle it with grace and confidence. When it comes time for you to leave the nest, trust that I know you're ready to fly. Please accept this book as one of the greatest gifts I could ever give you.

My dear readers, I invite you to join me as I teach my daughters the lessons your fathers would have wanted you to learn. I intentionally wrote this book for women of all ages. There are sections that may not relate to you. However, I can guarantee there are areas that will touch every woman's experiences with men. Many of our children grow up fatherless, and this book is meant to assist where assistance is lacking. The real world is very unforgiving, and only if you're very fortunate do you ever get a second chance. That is why I choose to teach in a way that's not easily forgotten. You've got to understand it and absorb it the first time. Turning the page will change your life forever.

WOMEN HAVE ALL THE POWER

CHAPTER ONE

AREN'T YOU TIRED?

AREN'T YOU TIRED OF USING SEX LIKE A COUPON AT THE grocery store—giving it up and receiving what equates to be pennies in return? Aren't you tired of watching woman after woman sleeping with men just to receive the crumbs of their material wealth? Aren't you tired of wasting years of your precious time with a man hoping one day he will ask you to marry him?

If you're not tired, I most definitely am. I'm tired of seeing our ladies, both young and old, making the same mistakes with men over and over again. It's a father's responsibility to empower his daughters with the knowledge necessary to be a successful wife, mother, and woman. This book will serve as a tool to teach you how to successfully deal with all aspects of men and relationships with them. In this day and age, so many young women are growing up without fathers and they are missing out on crucial development opportunities. Fathers bring balance to a child's life. I've heard women talk about how they don't need a man and they can do anything a man can do, plus some. Those types of statements are made out of sheer ignorance. The fact that men and women are different in just about every way possible is enough to tell us that our children are missing out on a whole lot by not having two parents in the household.

When boys grow up without a father, they don't have a role model for how to be a real man. They are surrounded by strong women but have no real sense of how to be a strong man. They don't learn how to be a husband, and they don't learn how to be a father to their own children. There was no one to teach them.

It's been said that a woman can never raise a man. Well, I'd argue that a woman can never raise a woman either. Sure, daughters will have a woman to look up to and emulate, but what kind of messages is she getting from a woman who has had to toughen herself up to be both the man and the woman of the house, both the mother and the father? Likely this female "role model" has been betrayed and hurt by men. Perhaps she has hardened her heart and become bitter. Or maybe she has been beaten down (figuratively and perhaps literally) so much that she's lost all sense of self-respect and self-esteem and she has become desperate for the least bit of male attention. What kind of example is that?

For sure, single mothers do a wonderful job with what they have to work with, but their children often grow up with holes in their personal development. When we are raised with two loving parents, we gain invaluable information that allows us to better deal with the opposite sex. We learn balance and how to deal with the ups and downs of a relationship. If you've never experienced downs, you can never truly appreciate your ups. This is why it is absolutely critical we do a better job of keeping our families together.

Heartache often goes hand in hand with the journey of love and marriage if you choose not to listen or learn from the examples that are put before you. But heartache is not a prerequisite to a woman having a successful marriage and a positive relationship with a man. If you want to take on a relationship without doing your homework, you will definitely be traveling a road riddled with potholes; however, if you're smart, you can choose to learn from other people's mistakes to make your road a lot smoother. There isn't a dating or marriage mistake you'll ever make that someone hasn't made before you. When you have a mother and father in the home, you are provided with an example every single day of what to do and what not to do. It's too bad so many women learn about men and relationships by trial and error. If you're patient and take the time to truly learn from all of those who have gone before you, your ride on the road to relationship maturity can be much more pleasant.

The fathers who choose to actively participate in their

daughters' lives have the opportunity to positively change it forever, just by sitting down and having the dreaded talk about "the birds and the bees." There are other fathers who are physically present but may choose to leave the subject to the mothers to discuss with their daughters. If your father falls into that category, at least you have the benefit of learning by observing his actions. The point is, I'm choosing to talk about all of those things that many fathers have difficulty discussing but know their daughters need to learn. Every man knows there are secrets, or "unspokens," that we discuss among the boys and that we would never discuss with women, but our daughters are the ones who need that knowledge the most. I've chosen to do something a little different with my daughters. I want to make sure they retain everything I have to share with them, so in addition to the lifetime of lessons they will learn from our conversations and the example I provide, they will also have the benefit of having it in the form of a book. This means they will have the ability at any time in their lives to pick it up and get a refresher course on these valuable lessons. I'm here now, but there is no guarantee I will always be here when they need my love and guidance.

When I started to write this book, I realized there are many women in our country who could benefit from the secrets I am imparting to my daughters. The lessons here are invaluable, and it doesn't matter how old you are; every lady on earth is someone's daughter and needs and deserves to have this information. As a matter of fact, some of the things I discuss are very unpopular with some of my male friends. One of them even said, "Man, do you have to tell them all that? If they don't know, they just don't know. It's one thing to tell your own daughters, but why do you have to tell the whole world?" That's when it dawned on me that I could actually be a positive influence on many women.

There are literally thousands of ladies, especially in the African-American community, who are growing up or have grown up without a loving father or male figure in the picture. Many of them spend their entire lives trying to understand men and understand themselves in an attempt to attain that fairy-tale relationship of which they've always dreamed. Many women are choosing not to marry. According to the U.S. Census, African-Americans are marrying one another at the lowest rate ever recorded. Imagine if you wanted to teach yourself to swim, but every time you got in the water you just about drowned. Pretty soon you'd decide swimming just isn't the activity for you. Many women have reached that point of exhaustion. They're just sick and tired of being sick and tired of relationships.

When I was dating, I could always tell when a woman didn't grow up with a strong male role model in her life. Many such women don't even realize they are giving off that vibe, but a wise man can spot it as clear as a neon sign. When an opportunistic man spots that trait in a woman, he knows it's going to be easy to take advantage of her. So many women today desperately need a man's love, but the only way they can relate to that emotion is through intimacy. That is why a father's love is irreplaceable. It allows our daughters to feel unconditional love and compassion without ever being physically intimate. Can you imagine how damaging such a lack can be for a young woman who sets out looking for love in all the wrong places?

The important thing now is to acknowledge the fact that there is an entire generation of young ladies whose only sources for information on relationships with men are what they get on the streets, what they see on television, and what they learn through trial and error.

Relationships between men and women are very complex, and the lessons I choose to share with my daughters, by and large, have a biblical base. Life doesn't come with an owner's manual, but I feel the Bible is the next best thing.

The Problem

America's approach to sex is too casual, which leads us to take marriage and relationships too lightly. It's one thing to date, have dinner, and catch a movie, but jumping around in the sheets with every Tom, Dick, and Harry who comes along has everything to do with why the divorce rate is so high. Infidelity is running rampant, and women are displaying more desperation than ever. Our society is suffering from a general lack of values and morals. I know that may sound a bit extreme, but it's absolutely true, and indiscriminate sex is the culprit. I know you're sitting there saying, "Now, how did he come to that conclusion?" Well, to answer that question we are going to go chapter by chapter and explore how this dynamic works. Sex is one of the most powerful forces in the world. Men approach sex one way, and women approach it in a completely different way. It is a multibillion-dollar-a-year industry, and it floods every form of media in this country—print, TV, radio, and the Internet.

Each one of the situations I mentioned in the opening paragraph when I asked, "Aren't you tired?" can be traced back to some deficiency in our upbringing. How we are raised is the source of our joys and, often, many of our pains. It is also the key to our emotional and mental development. If our homes are broken, then we as individuals are broken. And as go our families, so goes our society. The irresponsible ways we approach sex in our country can be directly correlated to the high number of unwanted pregnancies, the increase in single-parent households, and infidelity. Strong families yield individuals with self-respect, self-esteem, and high moral values. One of the most valuable gifts we can give our children is to teach them to have a strong allegiance to family and to set that example ourselves. The priorities in America have shifted; the desire for money, material things, and personal gratification have outshined the importance of focusing on our nearest and dearest. This also has led to a decline in morals and values. Family must come second only to God.

Although man was ordained by God to be the leader of his home, a good woman is truly the strength, the glue, and the backbone that allows a home to thrive. What use is a head without a strong body? Think about it. There are plenty of families who survive with shiftless husbands and wonderful wives, but how many marriages do you know that actually survive with a strong husband and a trifling wife? The woman is the most important ingredient.

Since women hold that cornerstone in the relationship, who is better equipped to change the disturbing trend of twenty-first-century dating and relationships? Women. Men tend to be more rigid with their emotions, whereas women are more pliable and adaptable. Women also have the God-given gift of persuasion—just ask Adam about Eve's gift. Do you think God would send the woman as a helpmate if she were not truly able to be one? I don't think so. I know I wouldn't want someone to be sent to help me who was no better equipped to tackle a problem than I was. When women start to realize their power and decide to take a critical look at what it will take to fix dysfunctional relationships, they will be much more efficient at putting their knowledge to work and producing a positive change.

You are the start of this change. Now, don't get me wrong; men have their areas that can use a complete overhaul as well. However, let's start with the gender that possesses the power to actually get the job done.

Right now our world needs your help to fortify our families by reinforcing our relationships. Since the woman's role is so important in this transformation, it is critical that you don't just go through life blindly and without a purpose. *You are important,* so take every experience as an opportunity to learn and gain wisdom because as a woman, you bring life to the earth. As the saying goes, "The hand that rocks the cradle is the hand that rules the world." You have that much power. To take full advantage of it, you must first understand sex and intimacy and the roles they play in relationships.

FREE WILL

Before I go any further, I want to remind you of a concept I've found to be very useful in my life, and I believe it can be useful for you as well. Free will.

As a father, all I can do is teach the difference between right and wrong, guide you through your mistakes, and lead by example. It's up to you to make your own decisions and to proceed in the proper direction. That's the way God treats us, and if it's good enough for God, it's good enough for me. The Bible teaches you the right way to go about doing things, but God always gives you the option of exercising your own free will. Again, Adam and Eve are a great example of this. However, there is a catch. If you choose to exercise your free will against what God has already designed as the right way, you've got to prepare yourself to deal with the consequences of your decision. As a father I can't do any more than what God would do. If you choose to exercise your free will in opposition to my better judgment, be prepared to suffer the consequences. As the saying goes, "Don't do the crime if you can't do the time." Parents always want to be there to keep their children from making the wrong decisions, but that's just not the way life works.

Earlier, I mentioned sex was the culprit for many of the problems we're experiencing in our society. Well, I bet you can probably imagine I will be talking a whole lot about sex and intimacy throughout this book, and I promise not to disappoint you. I'm going to discuss some other important concepts as well, but they all eventually lead back to sex. With that being said, here's my perspective on the whole sex thing: *I highly suggest you abstain from sex until you are married.* I sincerely believe that if you choose to wait until you are married to have sex, you will have a much more pleasant experience in your relationships with men and with marriage. Younger women are just not prepared to deal with the circuit overload that follows. Trust me, you are not mature enough to deal with all of the changes your mind and body will experience afterward. I'm even willing to put my neck on the line and say most women, regardless of their age, do not handle the emotional meltdown that follows premarital sex very well.

What do I mean by *circuit overload* and *emotional meltdown*? Have you heard women say, "Girl, he rocked my world?" Well, for most women sex "rocks their world" in more ways than one. And it's not the physical act that overloads their circuits; it's the difficulty they experience with the state of their emotions and their ability to further grow the relationship that causes the problems. Ask any woman if she has ever had sex and gone off the deep end emotionally. Almost all of them will tell you emphatically, "Yes." After you have sex, your expectations change, your feelings change, and the relationship you had will forever be different.

In contrast, sex for many men has no more emotional weight than going to the gym for a thirty-minute run on the treadmill. Now, don't get confused. Men enjoy it just as much, if not more, than women do, but when it's over, it's over. That is why I suggest you use your free will to abstain, even when everything you see around you is telling you to go for it.

The Power of a Woman

I believe the world revolves around women, mainly because just about everything a man does, he does with a woman in mind. He may try to tell you that's not the case, but it is. Men like nice cars because driving one catches women's attention. They get a good education to make a good living because they know women value security. Some men's sole reason for going to church is because large numbers of women hang out there.

Now, if a man is going to go through all of that in order to get your attention, why do so many women act as though the man they're dating is like the last twelve-dollar pork chop on the grocery store shelf? Judging by the images I see of today's women, it's apparently desperate times. I remember the days when a man had to court a woman. He had to prove to her—and her family—that he was worthy of her attention. A woman would have many different men who would do just about anything to persuade her to choose him. I know you don't remember those days because nowadays you've got women who just sleep with all of them and see who rises to the top.

But ladies, you possess a great power. Think of a man as a beautiful grand piano. When played by an untrained hand, all it produces is noise. However, when it's stroked by the hands of an expert, the results are incredible. I'm going to teach you how to be a master pianist and get the best out of your man.

The Blame Game

Too many women attempt to blame men for their relationship woes. If you let women tell it, they'll try to make you believe they've got it all together and would have no problems if their man would just act right. I actually get tired of hearing these same old complaints: "My man cheated on me." "My husband abused me." "This other man was on the down low." "All men are dogs." Don't blame men every time you come up short in a relationship. If you're looking for someone to blame, start with yourself. A man can only do what you allow. If you allow nonsense, then nonsense is what you'll get. If you demand respect, respect is what you'll get. Remember, you're the deejay of your own party. All the fun and games are over when you stop the music.

The other thing I hear women say all the time that really works my nerves is "There aren't any good men out there." There are plenty of good men. The problem is you don't know your own powers, and this leads to bad decision making. Think about how many young women you know who choose men based on things that don't matter. They pick a man because he's fine or because he's got a nice car. I've heard it all: "Girl, I'm going to get with him because he's got good hair." "I like him because he's a roughneck." What? Are you serious? Remember what I said earlier: Choosing the wrong man can be a death sentence.

Before you can start making good decisions, you've got to look inside yourself and come to grips with two important things. The first is knowing what you really want. Many women don't really know what they want. I've heard women say they want a man who's a good leader, but then they do more fighting against the program than working with it. I've heard women say they want someone who makes a lot of money, then they complain because he's always working.

The second issue is the way you approach competition. Women are so competitive with one another that often they'll let a man mistreat them just to keep him out of the clutches of another woman. They don't want a man no one else wants, and there are thousands who are just as content to share your man. There's more on that to come. I'm going to teach you what to look for so you don't end up singing that same old sad tune.

Let me tell you how today's men are thinking and how they've evolved. Men are now feeling like they are the puppet masters. As long as they can keep you women in the dark and fighting among one another, they'll make you believe they have the upper hand. I don't want to see you get caught in that trap. There are men whose whole purpose in life is to see how many different women they can sleep with. I know guys who consistently sleep with three or four different women weekly. Now, don't go putting your hand over your mouth and think, *Oh my God, men are such dogs.* If a man's a dog, what does it make the women he's sleeping with? This happens every day. But guess what? It just means there are women out there willing to settle for it. There are married men who get more "kitty" than most single men. You know why? Because there are women willing to settle for it. I can't tell you the number of men who are unemployed or underemployed who sit at home and live off their wives' paychecks. I'll give you one guess as to why. If you guessed "Because there are women willing to settle for it," you are correct.

To be completely honest, I can't fully blame the men for their actions. Women have the ability to put an end to this craziness but choose to let it continue. If you sit down and ponder the whole thing for a moment, I think you'll agree that part of it is human nature. For example, you go to the grocery store and you notice a gumball machine with a price of twenty-five cents for one gumball. You reach into your pocket for a quarter, but all you have is a nickel. Just for grins you decide to put the nickel in to see if it will work. When you turn the knob, a shiny red gumball falls out. Now, would you run tell the store manager, or do you just continue to buy gumballs for a nickel every time you go to that store? I'd be willing to bet you would continue to buy twenty-five-cent gumballs for a nickel. Now, who's to blame: the system (the gumball machine) for giving you a twenty-five-cent gumball for a nickel, or you, for only paying a nickel when the sign clearly says that it costs twenty-five cents?

Some men use a very similar approach toward women. If the system will allow them to get their goodies for a fraction of what they're actually worth, they will continue to get as much as they can—and get it at a discount.

I'm determined to give you all the tools you need to exploit your power. If you choose to use them to find a good man, then that's what you'll find. I'm not talking about any ole half a man either. Your powers will allow you to have a real man—one with values and integrity. All you have to do is keep reading. Once you master your own power, you will be able to find all of the successful, strong, hardworking, good men you can imagine. Better yet, they will find you.

Not all women have problems finding good men. In fact, some women have mastered the art of "man-ology" (the study of man) and have realized they hold all the cards in the relationship game. You can be one of those women too.

I've called it "the relationship game," and in a sense, that's what it is. Let me explain: As I've said, you have the ultimate power to make a relationship stop or to move it full speed ahead. You've got the gas and the brake pedal right under your foot. A woman's authority to say yes or no to a man's advances must always be respected. Men learn that at a very early age. Consider this: By the time a boy is eight years old he has already started to figure out how to get a girl's attention. He may buy her candy, write a note asking her to check the box yes or no whether she likes him or not, or just hang around and pester her to death. Young boys hit and play rough with girls as a means of physical intimacy. It's a preliminary way to touch and feel a girl without it being taken as an advance. By the time a girl starts to realize what is going on, somewhere around the age of sixteen or so, men have already had the benefit of an eight- to ten-year head start. Men figure out ways to circumvent women's authority.

They come up with all types of plans, schemes, and techniques to get what they want, and ultimately that's what the "game" is all about—men figuring out ways to get what they want. You have to learn to play the game too. You have no choice. This is the game of life and the only way you can win is if you stipulate the rules by which you want to play.

Ultimately we must succumb to a woman's authority. It doesn't matter how big a man is, how much money he has, or how much influence he may carry. Take Shaquille O'Neal, for instance. At seven feet one inch tall and 325 pounds or so, when the referee—at five feet six inches tall and 120 pounds—throws him out of the game, does it matter who Shaq is or the fact that he's more than a foot taller and almost three times heavier? No. He's got to collect his stuff and get to steppin', no questions asked. That's because the referee understands the power and authority he possesses. You have even more power than the referee, especially when it comes to men. When your man tries to break the rules, be prepared to put him out of the game.

Most men recognize a woman's power and try to destabilize it at every opportunity. Men have been at this game since the beginning of time, and some have figured out how to play at a very high level. But regardless of their cunning creativity, a wise woman can always identify his strategy and put an immediate stop to his game.

Again, not all women have a problem harnessing their power over men. Some have refined their skills quite well.

While a man may feel he's holding his cards close to his chest, the wise woman has already arranged the game to be played in front of a mirror so she can see the cards he's holding. She knows what he's going to play before he plays it, but she allows him to think his game is tight. These are the women who have their doctorate in man-ology. A wise man honors a woman's strength and knows not to challenge the powers that be.

Have you ever wondered why some of the most beautiful, kind, and intelligent women can't buy a marriage proposal? While at the same time, women who are seemingly less desirable have men beating down their door? I've not only wondered myself, but I've had female friends ask me numerous times to explain this dynamic. The answer is simple: The woman who makes full use of her God-given power usually comes out on top. I can't begin to tell you how many times women have asked me to explain why men do the things they do. The answers can be found in the chapters that follow.

Men aren't nearly as mysterious as women make them out to be. As a matter of fact, men are painfully simple creatures, once you understand what makes them tick.

The Golden Rule

I've always understood the Golden Rule to be "Do unto others as you would have them do unto you." Well, that sounds cute and all, but another version I learned goes something like this: "He who has the gold, makes the rules." Now, let's just replace *he* with *she*. I really need to make sure you understand this because it's going to tie into every chapter of this book. Women have all the power because they have all the "gold." And since the "gold" gives you the power, it allows you to make all of the rules when it comes to how power is distributed in dating and relationships.

Have you figured out what this valuable pot of gold is? It's the cookies, the goodies, the kitty. The gold is sex. I equate sex to gold because it is one of the most highly sought-after commodities on earth, and men go to great lengths to get it. In many cases, sex commands even more attention than money itself. It's one thing to lose your material wealth, but some men are willing to risk their wives and children when they choose to cheat. Some even risk their lives as a whole by choosing to have unprotected sex with multiple people, knowing that sex with the wrong person can lead to disease and death.

I refer to sex as a commodity because it can be bought, sold, traded, or many times just given away for free. Like any other valuable commodity, women have the choice to keep it and let its value appreciate, or they can use it up. I suggest you use your free will and keep it. Men will desire you and value you more than you ever expected, especially in this day and age when so many women are giving it up with no conscience at all. I know it may be a little difficult for you to understand men are that crazy about sex, but trust me, it's all of that and then some. Women possess the gold, and gold is power. Don't let anyone tell you any differently.

A woman must use her powers subtly. You can't just go around beating every man upside the head with your newfound power. It's one thing to possess it, but it's a whole different thing to learn how to use it. Be careful when it comes to receiving advice about how to use your power. Always analyze the source before you take it as truth. Remember, your girlfriends will be the first ones to talk you out of a good relationship. What works for you and your man doesn't have to be validated by your girlfriends. A wise woman knows to stay out of her girlfriend's personal relationships and keeps her girlfriends out of hers. Wise men have learned to be leery of women who are always consulting their girlfriends as to how to approach their relationships. Why some women choose to take the advice of their girlfriends over what their man is telling them, I will never know. If you have a problem with your man, learn to communicate that problem with him.

Communication is one of the most important skills to learn if you want to have great relationships, but it's also one of the most difficult. If you could be in your man's head, and vice versa, the world would be a much simpler place. What kind of sense does it make for you to have a problem with your man and turn to the advice of your girlfriends? That is exactly why I'm taking this time to educate you. And don't depend on some quiz in a magazine to tell you how to handle men. All those publications barely scratch the surface by going out and interviewing men, which is exactly where you should have started in the first place—with *your* man.

Your girlfriends will try to convince you they are experts on men, but who would you rather learn from: a woman who thinks she knows what's going on in a man's head or a man who knows? Besides, you can't always trust what some of your girlfriends are saying because they're too busy trying to get your man behind your back. Only a man can have the knowledge to critique what works for him and what doesn't. Now, if you want to date women, consult your girlfriends, but if a man is who you want, you need to buckle your seat belt and listen up.

Women are often looking for a fresh new approach to dating—a surefire way to get and keep their man. The best remedies are usually the simplest. We are going to explore some new concepts and revisit some old ones. I promise to give you accurate information you can understand. I just need you to keep an open mind and be receptive to the things we're going to discuss. The goal is for men and women to communicate better and seek resolutions as a team instead of you getting together with your girls and having a pity party. Nothing positive will ever come out of the late-night sharing of war stories with your girlfriends unless a knowledgeable and wise man is willing to give a testosterone-injected opinion.

Now, you might not like everything I'm going to say, but I promise you it's the truth. If a little anger slips in by the time I'm done, that's okay, because sometimes it's anger that is the motivation behind change. There is no magic potion that will make your man act right, but once you change yourself, if he wants to keep you, a man has no choice but to change himself.

CHAPTER TWO

MAN-OLOGY

EVERY WOMAN WANTS TO HAVE A POSITIVE, ENJOYABLE, AND mutually beneficial relationship; however, learning how to get to that point is where the difficulty comes in. But your success starts with you. It's up to you to take control of your destiny. That begins once you've learned to take full advantage of your God-given power.

The next most important move for you to make is to acquire knowledge. Anything you want to be successful at requires knowledge. To gain that valuable insight, you've got to focus on the particular subject you're interested in. You must take time to learn everything you can about men—how they think and why they do the things they do. Men approach life differently than women in just about every way. Don't think for one minute that because something makes sense to you it's going to make sense to a man. After you've done your homework, then you can go out and practice what you're learned.

Some women begin sabotaging their relationship as soon as they meet a man. They focus too much on being a girlfriend or a wife instead of starting out by simply enjoying the friendship. Too often women want to size him up for a wedding tuxedo before they even get to know him; they're playing house when they should be playing it cool. For instance, after meeting a new guy you think has potential, don't try to gain his attention by being overly flirtatious and dressing too provocatively. All that does is stimulate the sexual juices. Allow him to learn to like you as a person first. Sexy classy always beats out sexy trashy. Many women use their sex appeal to attract men, but men tend to have more of a long-term attraction when they truly enjoy spending time with a woman as opposed to just sleeping with her.

If you stimulate a man sexually first, you've instantly put yourself in a less than optimal position, because now his thoughts are being controlled by the little head between his legs instead of the big head on his neck. That's also when all productive thinking comes to an abrupt halt. I know you're probably thinking, *No way. Something so simple can't possibly get a guy thinking sexually.* Well, it is what it is. It takes very little for the blood flow to be redirected from the big head to the little one. It's something of which you must always be conscious. You have the power to flip that sexual switch in the mind of every man you meet. Yes, I did say every man. It could be your professor, your employer, or the man at the corner store. That's why it's so important for you to learn about the inner workings of a man because you don't want your power to get you into trouble.

To help instill this concept in your brain, I want you to remember this simple phrase: "A man needs PIEACE!" That's my way of combining the spelling of P-I-E-C-E and P-E-A-C-E. A man needs both, not just one or the other. Let me explain. As I said before, men are painfully simple creatures. As a matter of fact, we are so white-bread basic it's almost embarrassing for me to even go into detail. Women often overthink men's actions because women are much more complex creatures. If you learn to tone down some of the deep womanly thinking, you'll end up right where the minds of most men reside.

Here's what you need to know: Most of the issues you may have with your man can be summed up by the absence of one or both of these elements—piece and peace. Now when I say *piece*, I'm talking about a piece of tail, or if you want to be formal about it, sex. This is the fuel that makes every man go. It runs a man's world in every way. Men will go to the edge of the earth for sexual intimacy. If they're not getting it, they're searching for it, and if they're not searching for it, they're thinking about it. If a man spent as much time making money as he does pursuing a piece, he would be filthy rich.

Peace is the other important element. There is no hidden meaning to this one. Men value the absence of confrontation. At times it may seem like that's not the case, but don't be fooled. Men love to brag about how "cool" and laid-back their woman is. Men enjoy women who don't give them a lot of grief. No one likes a drama queen. No one likes a pushover, either. Be sure you understand what I'm saying. Choose your battles and learn to overlook his imperfections. A wise man understands that when it comes to matching wits with a woman, he's ultimately going to lose. Men will also do everything in their power to dodge conflict with their women. If they can avoid all the tears and feeling like dirt, they will. Men do not like drama. I'll talk more about peace in Chapter 5. Just remember, whenever you're trying to find your way out of a conflict with your man, whisper to yourself, "A man needs PEACE."

LOOKING FOR MR. RIGHT

Now that we know some of the basic building blocks of a man, let's discuss some of the specifics. How do you find the good men? you may ask. Merely by keeping your eyes open. But you can't search for a good man if you have no idea what one looks like. There are plenty of good men, but a lot of women wouldn't recognize them even if they came floating from the heavens with wings on their backs. I can't tell you exactly what a good man is for you, but I can definitely tell you what he's not:

1. Someone who has no ambition.
2. A man who is not willing to work.
3. Someone who doesn't make an honest living.
4. Someone who disrespects you or physically abuses you.
5. A man who lies to you and has no integrity.
6. Someone who is more concerned about himself than he is about you.

That's just to name a few. I know it sounds very basic, but you'd be surprised by the number of women who have men who possess each one of those qualities. They just try their best to overlook them. You've got to find the characteristics in a man that are right for you. Get over the "cute" and "fine" thing. It's important to be physically attracted, but it should not be your primary criteria for choosing a man. "Cute" doesn't pay the bills, and it definitely doesn't put food on the table. Think about this: If you think he's hot, there's probably an army of women who have the same opinion. With that being said, are you going to have your lip poked out every time he's approached or flirted with by another woman? Is he one you can't turn your back on without wondering if he slipped your friend his telephone number? With every positive, there's a negative; be prepared to accept both.

If you ever get to the stage in your life where you're thinking there are no good men left, you'll have to go back to the basics. That means you need a change in the way you see the world—a paradigm shift. You couldn't possibly think that *all* men are no good, right? Therefore, start by looking for the positives first. You'll be surprised by what you'll see if you just open your eyes. But be careful of spending all of your energy on a man hunt. The more you look for Mr. Right, the more often you will tend to settle for Mr. Right Now. If you live life and love life, Mr. Right will find you. Learn to love yourself and others will be attracted to your light. Women go wrong when they start to size up every man they meet as possibly "the one." Men can feel that vibe of desperation and will run every time. If you continue to do the things you enjoy, he will find you. If you meet a man while doing something you love, you will instantly know you've at least got one very important thing in common. Whatever you do, don't make the mistakes so many women make of settling for any man with a heartbeat. It's always better to be alone than poorly accompanied. Notice I did not say *lonely*. *Alone* is a neutral, whereas *lonely* is a negative.

If you don't have any hobbies or you're just a homebody, you're going to have to learn to get out. Mr. Right can't find you if you lock yourself up in the house every day. You need to get out and find the fertile ground for meeting men. Now, don't get it twisted. All ground isn't fertile ground for finding a good man. When I ask women where they go to meet men, the most popular answer I get is "at church." Fertile ground? Possibly. But church can sometimes present a bit of a problem. For example, what if I tell a group of one hundred women that I buried a five-carat diamond ring in my backyard. Are you going to rush over to start digging? You might, but the odds of you beating the other ninety-nine women to a ring are not good. Many churches are filled with women just like you—single and looking. Many black churches struggle with attracting a large number of single black men. The ratio of single women to single men is usually greatly disproportionate.

You've got to participate in man-rich environments. Let me help you identify fertile ground for meeting eligible men:

Ways to Meet Men

1. Join a civic organization. Chances are, if he's here he's at least employed. Organizations like the NAACP, chamber of commerce, investment clubs, book clubs, and rotary clubs are all good places to meet positive men. Don't be afraid to join groups that have a high concentration of men. That's the whole point. I will also caution you, however, not to join an organization solely to meet men. Find a group in which you are genuinely interested. This

(continued)

way, you can also gain valuable knowledge and additional contacts.

2. Develop an interest in sports, sporting events, and sports clubs. Men love sports. We also love women who love sports. Before I go any further, let me warn you about this one. Don't try to fake the funk. Men can tell when you're really not into a game and are just going through the motions. Women who possess a healthy interest in sports hold a special place in a man's heart. I know that's a hard one for you to grasp, but trust me. Find two or three sports in which you can develop a sincere interest. Try golf, tennis, fishing, or skiing. Football is always a great place to start, mainly because it's the most popular spectator sport in America. If you just can't bring yourself to stomach a Sunday afternoon football game with your man, be savvy enough to show him you respect one of his simple pleasures in life. Force yourself to allow him the time to take in a game without complaining about him not spending time with you. Fitness centers are also great places to meet health-conscious men.

3. Join a travel club. Imagine cruising the Caribbean. You're in paradise and you run into a man who piques your interest. The ambience is already set. When you're on vacation, hopefully you're not distracted by work, cell phones, daily chores, or the errands of a typical day. You're in a situation where you can save yourself a lot of time and energy by spending large amounts of quality time together before you even get home. These organizations take numerous trips throughout the year, and group members often grow to be some of your best friends.

4. Enroll at a local college or university. Take a class and learn something new. Schools are filled with men trying to better themselves. A man with a little drive and determination is always a good thing. Colleges are filled with them. Trust me, men are just as thrilled as you are when you display a bit of drive and determination.

5. Take a trip to your local do-it-yourself store. Home Depot is loaded with men on any given day. As a matter of fact, they even offer free classes for you to learn how to do certain projects around the house. Who knows? You might meet a man who is skilled with his hands (I'm not even going to touch that one). Finding a man who's not afraid of a little manual labor can be a great thing.

If you paid attention to the places I named, you'll notice that even if you don't meet the man of your dreams there you will have gained something positive by at least participating. I purposely left bars and clubs off the list. Most men don't view clubs as a place to meet a good woman; they just go there to pick up women. It doesn't take a rocket scientist to figure out that you shouldn't go to clubs expecting to meet Mr. Right. Men hang out at the clubs to find a piece.

The bottom line is that if you want to meet a good man, you need to get a life. Get out and live. You only live once and you don't get a practice run. Don't just go to work, go home, go to church, and repeat the cycle day after day. The only man who wants a couch potato is the one who's a couch potato himself. Now, is that the kind of man with whom you really want to spend the rest of your life? You've got to stay active. Women who have a zest for life attract men in droves, like moth to a flame.

There's one more very important characteristic that exists in today's men that women need to be aware of. The fact that so many men in the African-American community are raised without the presence of a father leads to a number of challenges for the women they date later in life. These men will either strive to be what their fathers were not, or they will emulate the behaviors that their fathers displayed. Some are so traumatized by their father's absence that they vow never to allow their wife and children to experience what they did. Others take the opposite approach: They were abandoned by their fathers, so they feel it's okay to abandon their families. It's imperative that you figure out which man you have.

Ask him how he feels about his upbringing. Listen to him closely and observe his actions. Needless to say, you want the man who hated growing up without a father and understands the importance of a father's presence.

Just Because It Glitters Doesn't Mean It's Gold

Don't be impressed by the unimpressive. Too many women sell themselves short by settling for a man with an attractive exterior. A man who is overly concerned with himself and his material things has no room to value you. This is a dynamic that has always baffled me. Just because a man is good-looking, wears a shiny new suit, sports some Now and Later gators, drives a shiny new car, and profiles a new Rolex on his wrist does not mean he is a good man. As a matter of fact, that's usually the joker who can't rub two nickels together. What's wrong with the guy in jeans and a T-shirt, driving a Camry, checking his Timex to see exactly when his check is going to hit the bank? You're tripping over dollars to get to pennies. Never allow yourself to be impressed by a man's depreciating assets (cars, clothes, expensive rental apartment). That's just a reflection of his debt. If you're going to be impressed with material things, at least be smart enough to start with his net worth.

Watch out for men who spend money frivolously. I had a woman tell me how flattered she was when her boyfriend booked her a posh hotel room, filled it from corner to corner with freshly cut roses, and had an expensive dress lying across the bed just as a surprise to show her how much he cared about her. Granted, I'd have to give the brother an "A" for style and originality, but when I said to her, "Wow, he must be paid!" she said, with a glowing smile, "No, not at all. He's living with his mother right now, but he just really likes me." All I could think was, *This fool must have fallen and bumped her head*. I understand it may have been a flattering gesture, but don't reward a man with attention and praise for foolishness. Now, if he has no problem affording lavish gifts, that's another story. But if the brother is broke, you have to question his motivations (and his sanity). Don't forget, the piece is always in the forefront of a man's mind. He must use whatever tactics are at his disposal to get the go-ahead for intimacy from a woman. Applaud your man when he exercises good judgment. Don't reward foolishness. This brings me to my next point: red flags.

Don't ignore the red flags. Some women are notorious for turning a blind eye to the warning signs, even if they're staring them right in the face. Instead of those flags just sitting there while you ignore them, let me wave a few of them for you.

1. If your man is living in his mother's house for more than a couple of months—I give a small grace period—**RED FLAG.**

2. If he drives an expensive car, but rents an apartment—**RED FLAG.**

3. If he overaccessorizes—**RED FLAG.**

4. If your man wears more than one ring per hand, more than one bracelet per wrist, and more than one necklace per neck—**RED FLAG.**

5. If he is always the one who's overdressed for the occasion—**RED FLAG.**

6. If your man is constantly spending money on you without regard to price (i.e., clothes, trips, jewelry) and he can't afford it—**RED FLAG.**

7. If your man constantly asks to "hold" some money or expects you to pay while on dates—**RED FLAG.**

8. If he approaches you with a flattering, yet rehearsed line—**RED FLAG.**

9. If he says he has a job but can't articulate exactly what it is he does for a living—**RED FLAG.**

10. If he talks more about himself than he inquires about you—**RED FLAG.**

**You can't say that I didn't warn you.
Remember your power.**

Now, just because I described these ten items as red flags doesn't mean it's an absolute no-go item if you encounter one in your man. It means you should take a critical look before going forward. There's a saying that goes, "Young men speak of the things they are doing, old men speak of things they did, and fools speak of the things they're about to do." Don't be impressed by the unimpressive.

The Thrill of the Hunt

Relationships will always frustrate you until you understand this very important concept: Men need to be challenged. Men are aggressive by nature, and once we devour our prey, we're off on the next hunt. This means that once a man feels he has you effectively under control, he will move on to the next prey that presents a greater challenge. As a rule, you should be elusive enough to keep the hunter hunting and accessible enough for him not to quit. That means you should continue to live your life. Don't drop everything to be at his beck and call. Continue to spend time with friends and family. Demonstrate that you have a fulfilling life. Men look forward to sharing the excitement of your world, but that's impossible if you've made the man you're dating your world.

Society basically dictates that a woman should have a man on her arm. This additional pressure has changed some rules of the game. Once a woman passes the age of thirty or so, she is expected to be married and have a couple of crumb snatchers. What society thinks of you can best be revealed by the dumb questions people ask. I've heard people say things like, "What's wrong? Why aren't you married yet? What are you waiting for? You're so pretty. Why can't you find a husband?" I cringe every time I hear those types of questions. Don't let this pressure lead you to become the type of prey that lies at the hunter's feet. Better alone than poorly accompanied.

Do you remember me talking about how men had to court women in order to gain their good graces? Well, it's tough for men to do the courting if women are pursuing them with pit-bull tenacity. I know the word *court* is very old-fashioned and not necessarily hip, but it's what you should require before you give him your seal of approval. A woman's aggression works against a man's basic blueprint. Again, men are aggressive by nature, with animal-like instincts—they are hunters. What's a hunter to do when his prey basically walks up and lies down at his feet?

It's the same thing that happens in the wild. Let's say we take a lion out of his natural habitat and every day we bring his food to him. Now, years later, we put him back in the wild. Check out what happens: He can no longer hunt. He has become lazy and apathetic, and patiently dies because he is no longer accustomed to hunting for his own food. The same is true for men. They are so accustomed to women chasing them that they have become lazy and unwilling to hunt. Now, who created this monster? Women. And it's going to take women to fix it. Ladies, always maintain your dignity. A man will never respect you when he senses you'll stop at nothing to gain his heart.

I would love to leave that point right there, but I know I've got to go a little deeper. Never make life-changing decisions in order to be with a man you're not married to. By that I mean don't move to another city, change jobs, or change universities. Keep him hunting. I can't begin to tell you how many women have done this and come up empty-handed. This type of aggression rarely, if ever, wins a man's heart. "Just keep on living," as my mother used to say. If he is serious about you, he will do what it takes. He should start by putting a ring on your finger.

As a hunter hunts, he is very observant of everything around him. Therefore, it's great to show your man you have a variety of skills, but don't overdo it. Show him you can cook and clean and you can be the breadwinner if need be and that you can meet his needs both in the home and out. Just don't do it to the point that he comes to expect it. What you're ultimately trying to accomplish is to show him that you're a very enterprising woman, which reveals to him that you're more of a benefit to his life than a liability. You want him to crave those qualities you possess by not receiving them all of the time. Let him know, for instance, that you'll only cook every day for your husband. Show him you're willing to stand by his side—to a point. When he feels completely comfortable and content, you've lost him. You must keep some of the cookies in the jar. You want him to see the benefits of marrying you rather than keeping you merely as a girlfriend. These are the things that keep a hunter hunting. He can think you're the finest thing walking the earth, but if you become the aggressor, taking his rightful place, he will divert his attention elsewhere. A hunter will hunt a prey who hides, one who runs, even one who bites, but hunters never hunt something that's hunting them back.

You're probably saying to yourself, *I would never do such a thing*, but I am willing to bet you've done it or you're in the process of doing it right now. Here are ten tips that will help you keep the hunt alive:

1. Don't invite yourself to activities or complain that you weren't invited. If he had wanted you to go along, he would have asked.

2. Don't invest in a man by moving to another city to be with him unless he invests in you first by putting a ring on your finger. Now, how often have you heard of one of your girlfriends doing this one?

3. Don't use shameful attempts to pressure him into marrying you. For example, don't suggest going to look at engagement rings, don't introduce him as your future husband, don't put your friends up to questioning him about when he's going to pop the question, and never try to trap him by getting pregnant. When a hunter sees what he wants, he will go after it.

4. Eliminate the following phrases from your vocabulary: "Where is this going?" "I'm not going to date you forever." "When are we getting married?" "I might be pregnant."

5. If you've chosen to abstain from sex until you're married, don't change your mind for fear of losing him. Stick to your morals and values. If he truly wants you, he will stay.

6. Don't abandon your friends, hobbies, or goals in an effort to be with him all the time. Keep a healthy lifestyle. Many women find the man they think is the one and they drop everything to pursue the relationship. Don't do that.

7. Don't attempt to accommodate his every need. Leave something for marriage.

8. If you choose to make sex a part of your relationship, don't give up all the goods. Again, leave something for him after marriage.

9. Don't agree with everything he says. Freely voice your opinion. It's better to find out you're not compatible sooner than later. Besides, it's obvious when you're doing this.

10. Never start doing anything you can't continue doing for the duration of the relationship.

Remember your power.

One more attempt to drive this point home: Men are not content to acquire "the low-lying fruit." A friend of mine once told me that "Men can have hundreds of suitable apples all around their feet, but they're not happy unless they go for that big, shiny apple on the highest branch."

Always keep the hunter hunting.

UNDERSTANDING THE PLAYA

Some hunters hunt to survive; others hunt as a hobby. The playa hunts for the sheer sport of it. As the saying goes, "Keep your friends close and your enemies closer." Well, the same goes for men. Women are often cautious of the infamous playas, but these are the men you want to keep close. A man can't be a playa unless he has something women want. It could come in the form of money, power, fame, or just game in general. Keep these guys close. Study them carefully. Be mindful not to get caught up, now, because these are the very men who are capable of selling ice to an Eskimo and breaking down the most defiant woman.

Befriend a playa or two. Your goal is to gain knowledge.

Observe his actions. Chances are, you won't get much more than surface information out of him if he isn't comfortable with you. Be patient because he will be more focused on getting to know you better than allowing you to get to know him. A true playa never completely rules you out. You are always fair game. It doesn't matter if you've been friends forever or even if you're married. When you gain his trust, he will share more information than you ever cared to know. Take the time to pick his brain. Most playas are proud of their tactics and are more than willing to hip you to the game.

Playas have a way of derailing a woman's mental, emotional, and physical state. They know just what to say and do in order to obtain their objective. Contrary to popular belief, a playa's objective isn't always about having sex with a multitude of women; it's about knowing he could if he wanted to—the thrill of the hunt. Ultimately, a playa's MO is about control. He wants his kryptonite to beat down your God-given power. He wants to get you to do the things he wants you to do, when he wants you to do them. I've seen women buying men everything from cars to jewelry to clothes. I've seen some of the most successful, beautiful, and strong women be completely dumbfounded as to how they became so blinded by a man.

He arms himself with charm, charisma, and a huge dose of confidence. Many women get caught off guard because they expect him to be easily identifiable—tall, dark, and handsome with a body like LL Cool J. However, playas come in all shapes and sizes. You can spot one by his charm that attempts to disarm. Be careful not to fall into his trap. Just observe. Your goal is to understand the man you're working with and to make good decisions once you've learned what you've got. The sooner you acknowledge your zebra's stripes, the quicker you can stop treating him like your prized black stallion.

Here are a few playa secrets every woman should know. I know a few men who are going to hate me for revealing these, but my daughters have a right to know.

1. The playa's cell phone rings while the two of you are in the car. He looks at the caller ID and realizes it's one of the women he's been hanging out with on the side. What's a playa to do? He knows he's going to have to answer or it's going to look fishy, so he picks up the cell phone as if he really answered it but he actually sends the call to voice mail. He then answers as if he were talking to one of his buddies, "Ah, man, I ain't doing a thing, just hangin' with my baby." Simple, but it works. You've got to be alert.

2. If you allow yourself to indulge in sloppy seconds by dating a married man, don't fall for the age-old trick of him expressing how miserable he is and him promising he's going to get a divorce. Yes, married men have mad game too. He wants to get you in bed

without putting his family in jeopardy, so this playa attempts to find a woman who has just as much to lose as he does, which is what makes this strategy work. He wants to know you're just as motivated to keep things on the low-low as he is. If you're married too, that's a plus; if you're successful, that's a plus. Anything that makes him think that he can get some without you showing up on his family's doorstep is a plus. Don't be a sucker—just wait until he's actually divorced. But I suggest finding someone else before you end up just like his wife—cheated on.

3. This is the silver bullet used to slay the woman who truly thinks she's "all that." This playa secret works best for men who possess a huge amount of confidence and have a bit of a swagger about themselves. Here's how it works: The playa targets you as his prey. He knows you're a woman who might be a little hard to get just by the classy way you carry yourself. All that does is increase his desire to conquer. He approaches you with sheer charm and genuine interest—no lines, no looking you up and down, no crap. His goal here is to subtly show interest without you fully understanding he is crazy about you. Time is of the essence on this one—whether you meet on the telephone, meet at the office, or are introduced by a friend, it doesn't matter. He must show he is kind, charming, success-

ful (i.e., he's got it going on), and most importantly unimpressed with your beauty. Sounds simple, right? Well, here is where he gets you. He plays your competitive nature against you. After he makes you think he's got it all going on in his world, he then proceeds to completely ignore you and act as if he is totally not interested in anything more than a platonic relationship. *Bam!* Now a woman's competitive nature starts to kick in, and she wonders why he's not interested in her. Beautiful and successful women are so used to men badgering them to death to show their interest that when a man doesn't beg, grovel, or drool all over himself, it's a blow to their confidence. Don't fall for this one, either. If he really wants you, he'll come back to make a more concerted effort.

Remember your power.

Now, when you find out that your stallion is a zebra after all, it is critical not to raise a whole lot of sand about it. The playa will be the playa, regardless of how upset you get with the fact that you're not his only woman. Displaying your anger will do nothing more than get your own blood pressure up. He will always have an excuse, so why go to battle? Juggling women is just what a playa does. This is exactly why you don't want to get intimately involved too soon. The right decision is just to move on. Never waste your time trying to change him, or any man for that matter. It drives me completely crazy when a woman is given all of the clues but chooses to stick around because she feels that she can heal a man of his playa ways. Again I say, move on. It goes back to that old saying, "Don't hate the playa, hate the game."

The Power of Suggestion

Think about the number of times you've driven up to a fast food restaurant and ordered a hamburger, fries, and a chocolate shake. You think your transaction is complete, but then the cashier comes over the microphone and says, "You ordered a hamburger, fries, and a chocolate shake, correct?" She then proceeds to ask, "Would you like an apple pie with your order?" Before you know it, you're driving off with an apple pie you never even intended to buy in your bag. This technique is called suggestive selling. Some men are absolute masters at using this skill to get women to do things they've never even imagined. Have you ever wondered how some men get women to buy them jewelry, clothes, and fancy vacations? The power of suggestion. Have you ever had a friend tell you about some wild, out-of-character sexual fling she had with a guy she barely even knew? The power of suggestion. Once you have a good grasp of this concept, you should never wake up in some man's bed scratching your head trying to figure out how those handcuffs hanging from the headboard ended up around your wrists the night before.

In fact, think about your first kiss, your first date, or the very first time you had sex. Some people might have a hard time remembering back that far, but I'm willing to bet you can identify times when suggestion led you to do something you never imaged yourself doing. This is why parents often disapprove of their young daughters dating significantly older boys or men. Grown women even have a difficult time recognizing when they have been a victim of suggestion, so a teenager has absolutely no chance unless she has wisdom well beyond her years.

Take note of the two following cases to better understand:

CASE #1

Trisha, a fourteen-year-old who has never even kissed a boy, meets sixteen-year-old Trevor in the lunchroom. Trevor, though not a bundle of experience himself, befriends her by striking up a conversation. Over the next month or so they spend time talking on the phone and getting to know each other. Trevor, driven by the same thing most of the male species is driven by—intimacy and physical contact—wants to move the relationship to the next stage.

He suggests to Trisha that they meet in the boys' bathroom so he can give her a kiss. Trisha's initial thought is, *Of course I won't*, but Trevor has just planted the seed by making the suggestion. Now Trisha is considering an act she has never thought about. All Trevor has to do now is continue to water that seed to get it to blossom into a kiss. Each day he does just that. Guess what ends up happening? Trisha meets Trevor in the boys' bathroom and gives him a kiss just as he originally suggested.

CASE #2

Alex meets Debra at a nightclub. They hit it off from the very beginning. They stand by the bar conversing and each of them has a couple of drinks—nothing major, just enough to allow them to release some of their inhibitions. Alex is very experienced at using suggestion to get what he wants. What starts out as a friendly, platonic conversation moves to exactly what Alex has orchestrated—a flirtatious encounter with hugs, touches, and kisses on the hand and forehead. He soon realizes she is just as attracted to him as he is to her, so he drops his first line of bait and says, "Wow, look at that full moon. I bet the beach is beautiful right now." She smiles and agrees. Alex then jokingly but methodically says, "One day I'm going to have sex with you on the beach under a full moon just like this one." She slaps him on the hand while laughing and says, "Boy, you are so crazy." The seed is now planted. Debra has these thoughts of having sex with this man she just met an hour ago now planted in her head. All Alex has to do now is make a few more suggestions before they're on the beach howling at the moon.

Suggestion is an extremely powerful technique men use to trick women into all types of things. Since women have all the power, men spend a lifetime learning how to circumvent their authority. Take the time to learn when a man is attempting to seduce you with suggestion. It's all around you. Some things are very innocent and harmless, but they can be used in the most devastating way. There are many unassuming women who get caught with this one every day. I've given you this tool, now be sure to make good use of it.

He Doesn't Necessarily Get Better with Time

It's important to understand that most men go through a playa phase, and believe it or not, it's actually healthy. The key for you is to be able to recognize when the phase has come and gone, or when it's about to begin. When men start to realize their marketability—why beat around the bush? When a brotha starts to realize his Mac Daddy appeal to women—it stimulates a number of changes in how he approaches relationships. This is where the term *sowing his wild oats* comes into play. Most men take a few years to experiment with the honeys and their newfound popularity.

When I say *Mac Daddy appeal*, this is the time when women start to notice him. This is when a man recognizes his magnetic pull—his sexual potency. His confidence skyrockets and he really starts "feeling himself," as the old folks used to say when I was growing up. This is when a man starts to develop that swagger. Let's keep it real; women are literally throwing the panties at him. If it were up to him, he'd get the biggest net he could find to ensure none of them hit the ground. All of this newfound attention allows him to fine-tune his skills. This is the time in his life when he starts to develop his trademark—how he approaches women, how he talks to women, how he flirts, how he kisses, and how he performs sexually.

Some women believe if they date an older, more mature man, they won't have to deal with all of the games and nonsense the younger guys are dishing out. They want someone who's faithful and not going to cheat, not going to be hanging out all night, blah, blah, blah. That belief can't be further from the truth. Let me tell you why. It all depends on the age at which he goes through the playa phase. Most men go through it, but at different times in their lives. For example, if a young man in high school is the quarterback on the football team, homecoming king, and he's cute, all the little honeys are probably jocking him. The panties are coming from all directions. This allows him ample opportunity to explore the ladies—yes, even in high school.

But here's the catch. Men can enter this stage at almost any age. Some are late bloomers. Imagine the creator of a dot.com. He was probably a computer geek throughout high school and college. The women probably paid him no attention whatsoever. But then he sells his online empire and becomes a billionaire overnight. Now check this out: he goes out and buys the fancy car, purchases the sprawling mansion, and changes his entire wardrobe, and now the women are coming out of the woodwork. He has arrived into the playa phase, large and in charge.

Now you come along, thinking that you've found the perfect man. He's forty-two years old, nice house, nice car, and dressed in a fine Italian suit. You're thinking, *He's got to be more mature and past all of the silly games.* Well, that's not necessarily accurate. This man has just recently moved into the playa phase of his life, and so commences a binge like no other. He will be getting more action than most sane men can even imagine. This phase may have been exactly what a well-known golfer experienced following the explosion of his popularity. Don't try to change him. This is a phase that you must let him transcend by himself—let that dog hunt.

Now you're back to square one, but you're okay because this education has shed some light on the situation.

Many men need to go through this phase before they can focus on monogamy. Remember what I said earlier about a man needing the piece. Be leery of a man who hasn't already been there and done that, because if he hasn't and his appeal to women changes all of a sudden, he will most likely try to explore to see just how far his newfound popularity will take him. When women start to pay him attention, it's going to be like eating Lays potato chips—he can't have just one. Men, just like women, must explore their sexuality. Men tend to go about it differently from women, primarily because they tend not to be as emotionally attached to the act. This is one of the hazards of marrying a man who is too young and not properly seasoned. A sexual encounter has no more emotional attachment for him than a workout at the gym. It's all about personal gratification.

Let me interject with a disclaimer here. I am in no way condoning these childish actions of some men. However, it is a mindset that is very prevalent, and something women should be conscious of. The only difference in a man who chooses to run through as many women as he can, and the one who is successful and content with just one, is discipline. Every man needs the piece, and every man is tempted, but it's the strong that take a more mature approach to relationships. It's a man's innate palate that oftentimes takes over his rational thinking. Women's knowledge of this dynamic will offer a more successful experience with men.

Man Logic

Not all men are playas, dogs, pigs, and whatever other name women use when their faulty decision-making gets them into trouble. Think about it. How many times have you heard, "There are no good men left. They're in jail, gay, on the down low, or they won't commit. They don't take care of their children." Men's shortcomings are vastly overpublicized, and women hear them so often they start to feed into that negativity. Granted, there are men who fit those descriptions. However, contrary to popular belief, the majority of brothers possess none of those qualities. Good men can be found, but it's very important you understand the logic a man uses to determine if you're the right woman for him. There are many different criteria he can analyze, but one of the more important ones is how you relate to him mentally. Men don't always want to explain why. They want you to be open-minded and tolerant of the gender differences.

I often hear women voicing their displeasure with men when they start to get frustrated with the whole dating game. Better decision making will help to curb that frustration. Doing your homework and coming to a couple of basic conclusions will help you understand men. First of all, you must listen to exactly what a man is telling you. Don't add anything to it, don't assume he meant something else, and don't try to change him. Second, it is absolutely imperative that you don't get hung up on what makes sense to you. Women like to attack dating and relationship problems by using woman logic, but many times that involves not believing him when he expresses his feelings. That won't get you to the relationship you're looking for. You need to take the approach of a police investigator. If you want to catch a thief, you've got to think like one. The same goes for trying to catch a man. You will never be able to relate to him by using what many women call common sense. When it involves your man, common sense is not so common—you've got to use man logic. Try to see the world through his eyes. Men and women are different in every way. We look different, we walk differently, we talk differently. Why would you even begin to think that using woman logic would get you the results you desire? You've got to think like a man.

Here's a major secret: When your man begins to express his feelings, listen to exactly what he's telling you. Women often try to get their man to express his innermost feelings, but when he does, he's rarely taken literally. Women, being the complex creatures they are, often think two or three moves ahead of men, and that's where the problem comes in. For example, a man can tell you one simple statement like, "I want to stay home tonight and watch the football game." To a woman, that can mean a number of things. Here's what a woman might think he's saying:

1. I don't want to be with you tonight.
2. This football game is more important to me than you are.
3. I'd rather you stay home because I'm staying home.
4. I have plans to meet another woman.
5. I want to go hang out with the fellas.

Your man is painfully simple. He's telling you what he wants or what he's feeling, so don't let woman logic turn it into something totally different. When he describes his views and what's important to him, believe him. Don't try to read into everything. Often he may not even know why he feels what he does, but you should learn to listen to exactly what he's saying.

Recognize the warning signs and move on, or learn to accept him the way he is. Trying to change him will only lead to a massive headache and heartache later. How many times have you dated a guy, recognized a fatal flaw, and continued the relationship because you thought that you could fix him? Stop trippin' and move on. No one is perfect, so the key is to understand your limits—your showstoppers—the things you know for absolute sure you won't deal with. Take the time and actually write them down. Once you know what they are, don't bend. Know what's important to you. It doesn't matter what your girlfriend may like or dislike; stick to your own set of guidelines. Never settle.

Keep in mind that there is a fine line between standing up for your morals and standards and being a quitter. You need to protect your heart and leave a man who is destined to hurt you, but I'm not saying you should walk away at the drop of a hat. One of the characteristics men value most in the women to whom they choose to commit is loyalty. It sounds simple, but you'd be surprised at how important it is to men. I've heard them say, "I need a soldier. I need a woman who will stand by me in a war." You have got to have your man's back. I'm not saying to be a fool and stay with a man who is not worthy, but it's important to understand how important your loyalty is to him. Men are usually less forgiving and take extreme measures to avoid getting hurt by women. This means that in order to truly gain his heart you've got to earn his trust. This need for a devoted woman comes in a time when loyalty is at an all-time low. The divorce rate is climbing, infidelity is common, and relationships are great until the first disagreement. Ultimately, men will treasure a woman who is loyal. This is why it's important to know just how much you're willing to take, and if he's worth your loyalty.

Overall, when it comes to men and women, every relationship will have its problems. Some are bigger than others, but it's important not to quit the first time you feel a little discomfort. It's a whole lot easier to enter a relationship than to get out, so take the time to make a good decision when choosing a man in your life. The best way to begin that process is by first learning about yourself. Know what is important to you and write it down. Also, write down the things you don't want to deal with in a man, then evaluate each one by asking yourself, "Now, this man has everything I desire but _____. Can I deal with it?" Even if he has everything you want, you should never bend on your nonnegotiables. Examples of nonnegotiables may be: drug use, a lack of trustworthiness, excessive drinking, a desire not to have kids, or even snoring. Figure out where you draw the line. Every relationship can endure the good times. The only thing that separates a good relationship from a bad one is how you manage conflict. Stand in your man's corner. Assure him you have his back.

Here's a real-life example of a woman not taking what her man is saying seriously. Most men really don't want to be considered a cheat. Really, they don't. But this is where man logic kicks in.

> When Karen and Larry first met, there was instant chemistry. Larry told Karen up front that he didn't want a relationship. They continued to go on dates, go out to dinner, and even dabbled in a toe-curling session or two. Eight months later, she was in love with him, and he was dating her as well as other women. He was living life with no stress. However, it was a different story for Karen.

> Her feelings for Larry were at their peak, and she wanted more. She really wanted to formally be his girlfriend.
>
> Karen and Larry were at a party together, when the discussion swung to relationships. Larry was asked if he had a girlfriend, and with Karen sitting next to him, his answer was emphatically "No." Karen was heartbroken. She ran out of the party crying uncontrollably and angry with Larry.

In Larry's mind he was completely within his bounds because he had told her from the beginning that he didn't want a relationship. He could do what he wanted, go where he wanted, and see whomever he wanted because he was honest and had told her up front. Many men use this approach, and this makes sense to them. As long as they aren't trying to deceive you, they feel that everything is okay. Some men choose not to commit because they want to see other women. If a woman chooses to sleep with him after he's already said he doesn't want a relationship, then that's on her. In actuality, he's not really lying or cheating because he was honest from the beginning. When your man expresses his feelings, believe him.

A man convinced against his will is of the same opinion still.

HANGIN' WITH THE FELLAS

It's important that you understand why men value hangin' with the fellas. This tends to baffle a lot of women, mainly because many women abandon their friends when they have a man. On the other hand, men like to hold on to their friends. I've heard of men actually turning down sex to go hang out with the fellas. Just because a man enjoys spending time with his friends doesn't necessarily mean there is a problem. If you take the time to pay attention to how men interact with one another, there are plenty of things you can learn about your own relationship. Having a firm understanding in this area not only will allow you to have a more productive and fruitful relationship, but will allow for a more restful night's sleep too. In just a minute, I'll give you a couple of pointers to get you started.

But before we dive too deeply into this subject, let's talk about the brothers on the so-called "down low." It's important that you recognize the signs of the men who are into this type of thing, but it's even more important for you to understand that it's the exception and not the rule. Women are taking this thing entirely too far. A man can't even walk down the street with one of his buddies without women looking at them sideways. Don't allow yourself to contribute to the negativity that is produced by those few wayward men (and I do use the word *men* loosely in this instance) who partake in that particular practice.

Here's a real-life example of how this stereotype can get in the way of making a solid connection with a good man. I had just started dating this lady when she asked me, "Have you ever been with a man?" I instantly took offense that she would even ask me about such nonsense, but I politely said, "No," and continued on to a different subject. Well, she wasn't satisfied with my answer and followed up with, "Well, why is Tommy always at your house?" Let's just say, my second response wasn't quite as polite as my first. Get real. If a brother is on the down low and a woman asks him that same question, what's he going to say? "Oh, why yes, sweetheart, when I leave this dinner with you I'm going to run right over to my man's house so we can get our freak on." Give me a break. We have enough wedges dividing our society; don't let this be another one. Learn to mentally account for your man's whereabouts. Don't badger him with unfounded accusations.

Here's an alternative to asking pointless questions: If you have the slightest inkling your man is a little light in the behind, move on. He probably is. Keep in mind that straight men do not regularly hang out with gay men. There may be some people with heated opposing views on this one, but hear me when I say that this is by no means normal behavior for a straight man. Your gut instinct is the best protection against this one. It's not even worth trying to ask him because he's not going to tell you the truth anyhow. As the saying goes, "You ask a stupid question, you get a stupid answer." Your job is to observe his actions and make a good decision. I shouldn't have to say it again, but move on.

In the traditional sense, it is very healthy for men to hang with the fellas. We do it because it's easy. This too may sound entirely too simple, but it is what it is. Remember, men are painfully simple. Hangin' with the fellas is how a man decompresses. It's a stress reliever. It's equivalent to the hours women spend pampering themselves at the spa, the salon, the mall, or the manicurist. Men use time with their friends to completely let their hair down. We don't have to open doors or pull out chairs in an effort to be the perfect gentleman. We can throw what little manners we have learned out the window. We don't have to watch our language, and we can communicate with each other in a language that we can understand. We can wrestle and clown around without worrying about being too rough. We can go out on the town without being asked the uncomfortable question "How do I look?" We can even gawk and comment on women's features without the fear of being slapped on the back of the neck. The time men spend with the fellas is an opportunity to recharge their batteries.

There's a saying that "Friends are the family you choose." Your man has family he has chosen in the form of his friends. Learn the characteristics of the friends he has chosen, and the knowledge you acquire can enhance your relationship with him. Men love women who can take part in their foolishness and exude a playful and relaxed disposition. Learn to go with the flow.

Observe the friends with whom your man spends time and take special note of how they interact. How he behaves with his friends can give you an incredible amount of insight on the types of people with whom he is comfortable. For example, if his friends (men and women) have low-key, type B personalities, that's probably something that makes him comfortable. If you know you have a high-strung, type A personality, then you can draw the conclusion that chances are, you're going to have an uphill battle with this man. The opposite is also true. If you notice that his friends are shrewd and opinionated, don't fool yourself into thinking you're going to reserve a place in his heart by being the sweet, innocent type who never has an opinion on anything. His friends are your clues to the characteristics he values in a mate.

Now if your man is spending an exorbitant amount of time with the fellas, that can be your first sign of trouble on the horizon. I know *exorbitant* can be a little subjective depending on the man and the circumstances, but if there is a distinct increase in the time he's spending with the fellas, start doing a bit of introspection. This can be an indication that he's cheating or that he's not happy with something that's going on at home. Women often seem to miss this one. Though men value hangin' with the fellas, there is a limit.

This one can be a little tricky, but remember a couple of things before you jump to conclusions. Men need to recharge their batteries, and they also need you to give them space without constant questioning and suspicions of cheating. With that being said, understand that if a man is going to cheat, there is absolutely nothing you can do about it. You can't be with him everywhere he goes, and you can't badger him to death with who, what, when, where, and why every time the door closes behind him. One of the biggest compliments men give their girlfriends or wives when talking to other people is, "Man, my girl's cool. She lets me be me. She's not always sweating me about where I'm going." I can't begin to tell you how much men value that characteristic in a woman. When you understand that you can't keep your man from cheating, it's better to trust him—not blindly trust him, but trust him until he gives you a reason not to. It's best to just observe. I keep saying *observe* because women tend to do too much with their mouths and not enough with their eyes. You'll learn a lot more by watching than by talking.

What should you observe? Watch how his friends spend their free time. Corner one of his friends and drum up a conversation with him from time to time and make small talk about some of the things your man shared with you about their last outing. You're going to have to corner him, because if there is really something going down behind the scenes, he will avoid having any type of drawn-out conversation with you. Your approach should be noninvasive, lighthearted, and open-ended. You don't want to allow him to give you a one-word answer. You want him to speak freely, because if there's ever a weak link in a chain of lies and deceit, it usually rests with the friend. For example, if they went to a basketball game the night before, ask, "What did you think of the game?" Then check out his nonverbals. Whatever you do, don't start probing with specific questions like, "Who did you meet? What time did you leave? Why did you go there?" This sort of questioning will definitely get back to your man, indicating that you suspect something fishy is going on. If you come across some inconsistencies in their stories, don't challenge him on it. Just keep a mental record. Do just enough to keep the lines of communication open with his friends. Observe the times they depart and return and whether the majority of his friends are married or single. Learn to be observant of everything that goes on around you—not nosy, but observant. Here are a few things you could observe, which you might want to give a little more scrutiny than usual:

1. He and his fellas regularly travel outside of the country without inviting their significant others.

2. He consistently makes himself unavailable or makes excuses for not communicating during the hours he is normally in bed—he left his cell phone off, had no

reception, couldn't hear it ringing. You should always be able to reach him.

3. He constantly tells you that he's spending the night at one of his friends' houses.
4. He regularly meets the guys for a drink after work.
5. His friends are mostly single and they consistently kick it at the club.

The bottom line here is that you should incorporate your man's friends into the landscape of your life. It will help you to gain a much deeper knowledge of how your man operates.

CHAPTER THREE

Stay in Your Own Lane

WHEN DID WOMEN STOP WANTING TO BE WOMEN? WHEN DID IT become so undesirable to be a wife and a mother? Why do women feel that they can do their job and the man's job too? Chivalry didn't die; women just decided they could do it better themselves. We've gotten to a point where women are taking on more of a masculine role in relationships, but then they are perplexed when men choose not to commit to them. In order for a man and a woman to come together as a team, a unit, a family, they both need to understand the importance of complementary attributes. A man needs to be a man, and a woman needs to be a woman.

I remember the days when young girls would play with dolls and dream of the day they would become a wife and a mother. Now it's become something they are ashamed to admit they want. What would be God's purpose in sending a woman to the earth if she were going to function in the same capacity as a man?

Do women solely exist as a toy for men? From what we're seeing today you might think so. This couldn't have been the way God intended it to be, could it? Until we come to the realization that men and women have separate and distinct attributes and we take pride in our differences and what each of us offers to the other, relationships will forever be contentious at best.

I'm not trying to weigh you down with the issues that are heavy on my heart, but I often wonder why more women don't recognize that this newfound independence and appetite for equality is a one-way ticket to nowhere. It's the cancer that slowly eats away at the fabric of relationships in this country. We're supposed to depend upon each other's unique skills and characteristics. A man needs you and you need him. We can never reach the full potential of our relationships unless a man accepts his role as a man and a woman accepts her role as a woman.

Men and women bring different attributes to the table, and neither set is more important than the other. We are not equal, but we have equal importance. This is exactly why you should never compete with your man. I think it's a shame I should even have to say that, but these days, especially in America, couples are competing with each other every day. Aren't we supposed to come together to make each other better? So, what's really going on? There shouldn't be anything a man possesses that a woman should desire to obtain through in-house competition, and vice versa. Couples are better off banding together in order to make each other better. Cutthroat competition has no place in the home. Women have been tricked into falling for the okie doke.

By pitting men against women, society has instigated a competitive spirit that's tearing families apart at the seams. It's impossible for a family to thrive in this type of environment. You don't have to prove your worth and importance to a man. Your job is to be the best woman you can be.

Let's look at a flower. It can only grow and blossom if it has ample sunshine and water. Water can't take on the attributes of the sun, and the sun can't take on the characteristics of water, but both are needed to produce a beautiful flower. The same is true in order for a relationship to blossom; a woman must be a woman and a man must be a man. Stay in your own lane.

Accept the fact that a man is supposed to be the leader of his household, to provide and protect. Now, just listen to me for a second before you get up in my face about this. This doesn't mean you're less than a man, and it certainly doesn't mean you're powerless. I told you, women have all the power. It just means that it's a man's responsibility to provide for you, protect you, and make decisions that are in the best interests of you and your family. You shouldn't accept a man as your husband, or even as your boyfriend, if you don't feel he can be an adequate leader of your household. It's a man's job to ask for your hand in marriage. And guess who gives the final okay? You do. If you don't have the confidence your man can be the leader of your home, find another man.

Remember, bad relationships are usually the result of bad decision making. You've got to look for a man who understands his purpose and takes pride in responsibly assuming the role God has appointed to him. Again, if you're with a man you feel you can't submit to—uh-oh, there's that word *submit*—then you're with the wrong man. Every time *submit* is mentioned, some woman screws herself through the ceiling by thinking that she is being asked to be subservient to some self-serving man. But the Bible assumes you chose a responsible, God-fearing man. Submission is only a bad thing if you don't take your time to find a man who's worthy.

I hear you saying, "I'm not submitting to no man. Who wants to voluntarily be a slave? Why do men have to beat their chest and claim they're in charge? I'm not going to serve any man hand and foot. He needs to be serving me!" You know, the hand on the hip, eyes and neck rolling, with the finger in the air never gets anything accomplished. The bottom line is that if you want a meaningful relationship, you're going to have to accept what's proven to work. A man must lead and you must responsibly follow. Think about this: Women have all the power, but they're the ones who are expected to submit. Hmmm, now there's a concept. Well, it's exactly as it's supposed to be. It's called checks and balances. It's what keeps women from taking advantage and keeps them from being taken advantage of. Imagine the problems we'd have if men were the leaders and possessed all the power. I think you can see why that would be a problem. So why reinvent the wheel? Understand that relationships were designed to work this way. If your relationship isn't working, it's a sign you're probably not using your power correctly. As the saying goes, "Power corrupts, and absolute power corrupts absolutely."

A good leader does not demand respect; he earns it. If you know you've got a good man, give him that respect. Instill it in your heart. When you only have two people in a relationship—and that's the way it should be!—it becomes very difficult to make tough decisions because disagreements always end in a fifty-fifty tie. Someone has got to be able to break the tie. A great relationship is no more than a beautiful dance. The man leads and the woman follows. As long as the man is a good leader and the woman submits to her partner, they effortlessly glide across the dance floor. But watch the drama that jumps off when a woman tries to take control during a dance with a man who's a good leader—it's nothing short of disaster. Relationships work the same way. As my pastor used to say, "The only thing I know of with two heads is a monster."

I want to make sure you didn't miss the most critical

point of this section, so let me break it down in case you did. I just made two statements I don't want you to skim over. I said, "Submission is only a bad thing if you don't take your time to find a man who's worthy." I also said, "As long as the man is a good leader and the woman submits to her partner, they effortlessly glide across the dance floor." If the man is not a good leader, the dance is also doomed. In short, you need to find a man who's worthy of your submission, and one who's a good leader. Whether you can submit determines whether you can commit. If you feel that you're unable to submit, regardless of how cute he may be, that's not the man to whom you should commit. Not all men are worthy of your submission, but all good relationships require it.

However, good leaders are hard to come by. When women start to demand leadership from their men, men will have to adapt and develop better leadership skills. It is absolutely essential that you find a man who is a good leader and that you possess the authority to appoint him. Take that whole fifty-fifty concept and trash it. Good relationships are not fifty-fifty partnerships. That's a broken-down theory that has no merit. Every team requires a leader. A good leader doesn't divide duties and split them evenly. A good leader delegates to the person who is best equipped to produce a favorable result. He should be logical, levelheaded, and charismatic. He should be knowledgeable, humble, and a good communicator. He should know how to motivate and how to discipline. Your man should have these skills. If he's a good leader, he will not use his position irresponsibly; he will make selfless decisions that benefit the family first. He will lead by example and should never treat you like a slave. If he treats you this way, then I'd venture to say you made a bad choice, and that's exactly what I'm trying to prevent you from doing.

I challenge you to put the leadership ball back in your man's court. I guarantee that you will get results you never imagined were possible. Just do your part as a woman and always have your man's back. A softer, less aggressive approach will get you much better results than being controlling and overbearing. Compassion and understanding begets compassion and understanding. If more women understood the effectiveness of subtlety, they would use it much more often. Show him you can be submissive. Challenging his manhood can bring sudden death to the relationship, and most men will not tolerate it. Display the nurturing spirit that is within you first. If that doesn't work, wait until cooler heads prevail, and then approach the issue again.

I overheard one man saying, "Some women come at you so hard you want to put up your fists. You forget they're even women. You feel like you've got to defend yourself as if she were a man. They just don't believe in submission." Always maintain your grace and dignity. If you use aggression and hostility in an attempt to get what you want, you will receive the same in return. Hostility begets hostility. Practice killing him with kindness. Before long, a good man will acknowledge your humility and will do everything in his power to match it. The more you try to do for him, the more he will bend over backward to lighten the load. Your kindness and willingness to put him first stimulates something inside that makes him want to do whatever is possible to keep you happy. Try it sometime.

Shoot for the Stars

"Michael, you keep saying I need to act like a woman. I'm a woman all day long. Are you trying to say I shouldn't use the brain God gave me? Are you saying I'm supposed to be barefoot and pregnant?"

I'm not saying that at all. However, I do feel that now is the time for women to embrace everything that makes them different from men. Our communities can't truly prosper as long as the family is taking a backseat to materialism. You can still aspire to be an astronaut, a race car driver, or an Indian chief, but that doesn't mean you should neglect your role and responsibilities as a woman. I would never suggest that anyone put their dreams on the back burner, but the family is the building block of society and should always be a part of your thought process. If you value being a wife and a mother, but can't maintain your responsibilities because of your occupation, career, or pursuit of your dreams, you probably need to reassess your purpose in life.

There's no man who's going to give you an extra-special place in his heart for showing him you can perform in your career field as good as or better than he can in his. Quite frankly, that actually means nothing to him when it comes to choosing a mate. I understand not all women even desire to have a family, and that's okay too, but if you think one might come in handy at some point in your life, you might want to keep these thoughts in mind. In actuality, what is life without someone special to share it with? Balance is something all of us should strive to achieve.

As more and more women enter the professional workforce, they fall prey to the stigma society places on women who perform in more masculine roles. Society would have you believe that you need to conduct yourself as a man would when you take a position traditionally occupied by men. That is so not true. As long as your performance equals or exceeds that of men, why should anyone attempt to make you conform to a more masculine standard? Never lose who you are. Embrace your femininity. Don't hide it. Take Florence Griffith Joyner for example. "Flo Jo" was a pioneer in changing the psyche of female athletes around the world. Most of the female athletes of the time chose to keep a thin veil over anything that was too feminine, but she dared to be different. She captured the world's attention at the 1988 Seoul Olympics by setting a world record in the 100-meter and 200-meter dash, complete with painted fingernails, makeup, and her own femininely designed track outfit, not to mention hair that looked salon fresh. What set her apart is the fact that she embraced her femininity in an arena where it wasn't the popular thing to do. Look at the impact she's made on many of today's athletes, almost twenty years later. Tennis players Venus and Serena Williams, race car driver Danica Patrick, golfer Michelle Wie, boxer Laila Ali, and many others are products of Flo Jo's bold stance.

Society has also pressured women into suppressing some of their other most endearing feminine characteristics such as displaying emotional tears, exhibiting compassion, and nurturing others. It appears to me that women are feeling they can't express themselves emotionally because they are led to believe it's a sign of weakness. I don't believe that. We need more of our leaders to possess those traits. Those are the characteristics women use to influence every man who has ever had a leadership position. The majority of all the male leaders in this country are married. Don't think for a moment their decisions aren't greatly influenced by the woman standing at their side. If a female held a similar position in society, why would it be inappropriate for her to display emotion? Can you imagine what the world would be like if everyone felt they had to mask their inner feelings? I'd say it would be one sad place to exist. A woman's emotional, caring, compassionate, and empathetic nature brings balance to a man's more stoic one. Everything must work together in perfect equilibrium.

The same goes in a relationship. A man wants a W-O-M-A-N. Don't feed into the hype of masking your emotions in an effort to appear strong. That entire notion came about as a result of the women's labor movement. Leave that nonsense at the workplace. Men want and need women to be softer emotionally. Men don't necessarily understand all women's emotional peaks and valleys, but they can definitely do without an emotionless rock. Women who present a stonelike exterior, as if to show indifference, run men off. You may feel you're being strong or protecting your feelings, but it comes across as uncaring in a man's eyes. No matter how you look at it, men are affected by women's emotions. It allows them to draw closer to the women they care for.

Stop trying to brush your femininity under the rug. If you want to be a good mother and a good wife, just do it. If you choose to be a race car driver and you want your car painted pink with a floral hood, just do it. If you choose not to ever work outside of the home, just do it. Don't allow society to dictate how you're supposed to live your life. And whatever you do, don't allow your role in the family to suffer as a result of the pursuit of your dreams. Cherish your femininity and find balance in your life.

Old-Fashioned Is Hip

I remember a time not too long ago when a man had to know a thing or two about chivalry to get the woman he wanted. In order for him to be deemed worthy of a good woman's attention he had to come correct or go home. Women insisted that a man open the door for her, help her with her coat, and pull out her chair when she was ready to sit down. There was never a question as to who would pay the tab on dates—that was what a man was required to do. If she was cold, a man would offer his jacket. If a woman was carrying something heavy, a man was expected to take it off her hands. If her car broke down on the side of the road, he'd better be prepared to either fix it or push. If a burglar was heard creeping around the house, a good man was prepared to take the first bullet. I say all this to remind you of the way women used to run the show and how men graciously complied with their demands. Men went along with the program willingly because they understood the value of a good woman. In return, women would perform their traditional role in order to keep their man happy.

Now here's the rub: Many of today's women still expect men to display their chivalrous spirit, as they should. Most men know that going in and try their best not to disappoint. But let a man twist his lips up to ask today's women to cook for him regularly, wash his clothes, or to stay home and take care of the kids? No way. Better yet, imagine the reaction a man would get by going to his lady's house on the first date, sitting down, and expecting her to prepare him a plate of food. He better not even think about asking her to bring it to him. She'd rather run through hell with gasoline panties on than let that happen without a fight. The mere thought of the wrath to be unleashed should be enough to motivate him to just get up and do it himself. I've seen it happen. I've even seen mothers trying to help out, saying, "Girl, you're not going to fix that man a plate?" Then comes the eyes rolling and, "What's wrong with his feet? What do I look like? He's got two arms."

Too many women choose to embrace traditional roles only when it's convenient for them. You can't have it both ways. I'm always amazed by the number of women who judge the quality of a man by how he performs his traditional duties. I don't have a problem with that at all. I think that it's a good place to start, but I'm equally amazed by how offended some women get when men judge them by that same standard. To be treated like a lady, you've got to act like one. A real man who is a leader and provider and who understands the role he is to play in a relationship will demand that you know your role as well. So choose what side of the fence you want to stand on. If you want a man who works, don't be offended if he expects you to care for the kids. If you want a man to fix things around the house, keep cars clean, and keep the grass cut, don't get bent out of shape if he expects you to keep the inside clean. It's the only way things can run smoothly. It's all about being able to dance beautifully together, right? Old-fashioned values are in style.

That brings me to my next point: cooking. Men know *cook* is a four-letter word, but there are plenty of other four-letter words that bring less of a reaction than a man letting this one roll off his tongue. When you prepare a man a meal, he doesn't just see it as the same meal he ate yesterday at Sizzler. He views it as one of the most kind and giving gestures you could possibly offer. It's right up there with sex. That old quote "The way to a man's heart is through his stomach" still carries a whole lot of weight, even today. It is important. It plants the seed in a man's head that you're capable of taking care of a family. It demonstrates those caring and nurturing qualities. If you choose not to carry on any other traditional trait, consider keeping this one. The mere thought that you took time out of your day to think about what he might like, went to the store, and bought it, prepared it, and then cooked it is the ultimate nurturing gesture. Cook for your man. If you can't cook, learn to. At the very least, show a genuine interest in seeing to it that he is fed, even if it means regular trips to a restaurant to buy it. Bring it home and put it on a plate. He'll still appreciate the effort. If you don't typically cook, try it, and watch the response you receive.

One lady recently said to me, "I don't need to cook for

my man; he enjoys doing the cooking. As a matter of fact, he's always inviting me over for a home-cooked meal."

That's all well and good, but you need to recognize where that came from. Today's man has a choice: either learn to cook or starve to death. A woman who is willing to cook for her man is becoming as rare as a Jheri curl. Most of my friends, both married and single, eat out just about every day.

True story: One day years ago I was eating breakfast in my favorite restaurant when my mom called on my cell phone. She said, "Hi, baby. What are you doing?"

"Oh, I'm in the same place I usually am about this time, eating at IHOP."

She said, "Boy, I can't believe you eat out every day. You need a wife."

I responded back, tongue in cheek, "For what? All that would mean is that I'd have to pay for two meals at IHOP."

I just thought I'd throw that in to solidify the point. You must get in the habit of cooking for your man.

Married men aren't doing much better when it comes to getting a freshly cooked meal consistently. If you're not working outside of the home (I've got to be careful how I say that, because if I were to say, "If you're staying at home and not working," I'd get this look from the depths of hell, followed by, "Being at home is work! I've always got things to do," so I'll go ahead and admit that I've been beaten into submission), why can't your man have a home-cooked meal when he comes home from work? It sounds rather unbelievable that married men can't get a home-cooked meal after work while their wives have been at home all day, but here's an unfortunate story from a friend of mine showing just that.

I'll call him Joseph. After Joseph got married, he gave his wife a choice: She could either stay home or go to work after the birth of their first child. She chose to stay at home. Now, I think it's safe to say that if you volunteer to stay home and your husband is hitting the job ten to twelve hours a day and you only have one child, there should be no reason for him not to have a home-cooked meal when he comes home, right? Well, Joseph would often come home starved after a long day's work only to find that his beloved wife, who'd been home all day long, just didn't have time to cook dinner.

He should have gotten the hint early on when he arrived home from work and observed the first sign of trouble: The kitchen smelled like Pine-Sol. Since there were no pots and pans on top of the stove, he proceeded to think, *Oh, she must have put dinner in the oven for me*. He opened the oven door, and again, nothing in there but the smell of Pine-Sol. *Well, I am kind of late. She probably put it in the fridge already*, he thought. The tension mounted as he eased open the refrigerator door. He looked in and realized that she had been home all day and hadn't taken the time to even throw some Vienna sausages on a plate. And to top it all off, that Pine-Sol smell was from the previous night when he had cleaned the kitchen. You'd be surprised at how many men have stay-at-home wives who don't even cook for them regularly.

All I'm trying to get you to understand is that you can't expect a man to embrace his traditional role if you're not willing to embrace yours. Notice I keep saying, *embrace your traditional role*. If you do it because you feel you have to, you might as well stick to what you were doing before. You can't fake it, because eventually the dust will settle and he'll realize he's been hoodwinked. If you do it because you understand in your heart that a man and a woman must each do their part, you will have a long, successful relationship. The truth is, for men this is truly one of the characteristics that separates a woman you date from the woman you marry.

Here are ten "nevers" that every hip, old-fashioned woman should practice while dating. (When I say *dating*, that means you have not made an exclusive commitment to each other.):

1. Never ask a man you've just met for his telephone number. It's okay to give him yours, but wait until he calls you to ask for his. Asking for his number shows aggression on your part.

2. Never pursue a man or ask him out on a date. It's too forward and reveals a hint of desperation.

3. Never pay on the first few dates, but always periodically offer and be prepared to pay every now and then. Men tend to look favorably on women who are willing to treat from time to time.

4. Never invite a man into your home and never go into his home until you have gone out and spent numerous dates in public places. This just provides a layer of safety when you're on a cold date (meaning you have no background or history on the guy you're going out with). If you've known him for a significant amount of time and then just decided to go out on a date, that's different. Always let a friend or family member know where you're going on a cold date, and give them as much information as possible.

5. Never allow a man to honk his horn in order to pick you up from your home. He should always come to the door and take you back to the door. It sets the standard for how you intend to be treated.

6. Never kiss a man on the lips on the first date. I hope it's understood that you should not sleep with him on the first date either. Kissing on the first date simply rolls out the red carpet for escalating intimacy on the

dates to come. You must keep his sexual juices on lockdown and focus on the friendship first.

7. Never ask a man for money. Simply put, it's tacky. Ask a family member or a friend you're not dating if you need financial help.
8. Never be too accessible or readily available. It gives men the perception that you have no life. Men like to share in your activities. And in order for the relationship to move in a positive direction, you must present a small challenge to him.
9. Never ask a man how much money he makes. Nothing good can come from that question. If he makes a lot of money, he will be suspicious of your intentions. If he doesn't make a lot of money, he will feel that he doesn't measure up. My follow-up question when a woman asks how much I make has always been, "Why?"
10. Never forget who truly has the power.

It's a Small World after All

The traditional approach to relationships may seem a little outdated, I know, but the reality of the matter is that people in the majority of the world operate by these traditional values, and I believe they've got it right. I've had the luxury of visiting almost every major city in the world, and I can honestly tell you that we Americans with all of our self-righteous thinking have it backward. The family unit is the most important aspect of society, but in America it has taken a backseat to materialism. The family is the schoolhouse for the soul. It's the foundation of our value system and the framework for our sense of loyalty and integrity. It's the main building block of one's respect for rules and authority. America is the so-called richest country on the planet, but riches can be measured in many ways other than monetarily. If you consider that our country suffers from a failing education system, an overcrowded prison system, an obesity epidemic, and a divorce rate that is among the highest in the world, I think some would not consider us to be so rich. All of these shortcomings of our society can be traced back to our fragmented families. A strong family foundation has proven to be the shot in the arm that builds more productive members of society. Maybe family values ought to be a little higher on the list of priorities in our country.

Changing our current track begins with making some sacrifices for the family's sake. Couples who choose to have children need a philosophy overhaul. Children need to be raised, and the only way that becomes possible is by spending quality time with them. I often hear how hard it is to make it off only one income, and that may be completely true, but if you can't afford to stay home and raise your children, change how you think of your need for material things. Reevaluate your priorities. Consider buying a smaller home, purchasing less expensive cars, or resisting the urge to buy name-brand goods. If you have to compete with the Joneses, have a contest to see who can spend the most quality time with their family.

I've found that most Americans who haven't done much traveling abroad have a distorted sense of reality when it comes to family values. Fortunately, I've had the opportunity to visit approximately fifty different countries. During that time, I couldn't help but observe how cohesive many of the families were. Whether I was in South America, Asia, or Europe, women there continue to make managing the home their first priority, while the men's primary concern is to work and provide for their families. Many of the women work outside of the home once their children begin school, but it is obvious that home is where their heart is. Work is truly secondary. The women run the home and all of its activities—clothing, feeding, cleaning, you name it. Even with such a large responsibility, they still seem to spend significantly more quality time with their husbands and children than we do in America. If you're not willing to make your home the center of your world, then reconsidering your pursuit of a family is probably in order.

The Beauty of a Woman

Women possess a God-given beauty like no other. Physical beauty is only one small part of a woman's total package, though. The way that you walk, talk, and smell, and the way you carry yourself in general are all part of your limitless package. However, some women have a way of voluntarily destroying their natural beauty and worth. Just close your eyes for a moment and try to visualize some of the women you've seen in your life. They've got tattoos, gold teeth, cigarettes hanging from their lips. Some curse like sailors, and some even act like men. Can they see themselves? Do you think they actually have mirrors in their homes? Why would any woman purposely destroy her natural beauty?

A huge part of the problem is the environment that surrounds these women. Many don't even recognize the problem because so many other women look just like they do. However, as those women mature, these flaws become much more apparent when they venture out of their environment into the rest of the world. I just want to point out that there are some women who can't find a decent man because they can't see that they're destroying their self-worth by trying to keep up with the trends, fads, and people of their surroundings. This can be a very thorny subject, I know. No one likes to be told their way of doing something isn't necessarily the right or good thing to do. However, someone's got to do it, so it might as well be me.

Quite frankly, some women just need to be more observant. They need to look out at the rest of the world. Read a newspaper or magazine or watch TV in order to pick up on some of the things to which men are attracted. Some of the ways that women conduct themselves should not be dependent on what a man thinks about it. You should develop your own personal standard of excellence. I know that may be a little challenging for some, so I'll help you out a bit. Start by changing the company you keep. Find people with a positive, healthy outlook on life. It's contagious. They should provide an environment that allows you to grow and develop new facets of life. New friends influence your life in just about every way. They can affect the way you walk, talk, dress, and think. Learn to separate the positive attributes from the negative ones.

This leads me to incredibly thorny point #1. Always maintain your health and physical appearance. Men are visual creatures. Let's keep it real. Physical attraction is often the first thing that catches a man's attention. He must first cross that bridge before he can see what's on the other side. If the bridge is in need of repair, a man may altogether miss the treasures on the other side. Call it shallow, call it superficial, call it a doggone shame, but it is what it is. You must present an attractive package. You always hear people say, "Beauty is only skin deep." Well, don't forget the other half that says, "Ugly goes to the bone." Each man has a different standard of beauty, but ugly ways tend to be universal. If you don't present a polished exterior, your beautiful interior may never get noticed.

Whether you're married or single, maintaining the allure that initially captured your man's attention is crucial. Some women are masterful at attracting a man, but haven't got the slightest clue as to how to keep him. Whereas other women have no idea as to how to attract him, but have what it takes to keep him. When you're done reading, you should have a healthy understanding of both.

Let me start by saying that men are always assessing your tendency toward blowing up. Again, call it shallow if you want, but it is what it is. You can have it going on, but if he detects an extended trip to Jenny Craig in your future, you may lose him altogether. A man is expecting you to be able to fit into that wedding dress for the rest of your life. Don't slip. He observes everything when it comes to your appearance, your eating habits, your muscle tone, whether you lead an active lifestyle, and even what your mama looks like.

Men do everything in their power to predict what you're going to look like in twenty years. If you were five feet seven inches and 120 pounds when he met you, and now you're 180 pounds, don't have your lip poked out when he's not as affectionate as he used to be, and don't be surprised if he would rather see you in clothes than out of them. The opposite is also true. If he met you when you were five feet seven inches and 180 pounds, don't all of a sudden choose to explore the effectiveness of the Atkins diet and lose sixty pounds. A man likes what he likes.

This is one of a man's greatest nightmares. He is dreadfully afraid of his beauty queen spending too much time at Dairy Queen and putting on those twenty-plus pounds of unwanted weight. Why would you even let it happen? It is critically important to maintain a healthy lifestyle, not only for him, but for your own self-esteem. No matter how old you get, eating right and exercising regularly can't be emphasized enough. If you have children, don't use them as a weak excuse for your weight gain. Push back from the table, put on your workout clothes, and place one foot in front of the other as you make your way to the gym. Think about it. When he leaves home he is being approached by women left and right who look like a million bucks, so why are you walking around looking like a buck fifty? Don't work out just to get him. You've got to stay fine so you can keep him.

When I talk to men who cheat on their women, not being physically attracted to her is one of the more popular excuses as to why. Whether it's truly the reason is not the point. Why even allow him that excuse? Women want their man to be loving, passionate, and romantic. If you're not visually pleasing, it's very difficult for him to fulfill your needs. It's his eyes that keep the love alive. Never let yourself get so comfortable with your relationship that you start taking your appearance for granted. How you feel about yourself when you have no clothes on will glow like a neon sign when you're wearing clothes. I see it all the time. When you first got together, you would keep a healthy supply of Victoria's Secret lingerie, but it only takes a couple of years before the underthings from Victoria's Secret are long gone. All he can look forward to is the hair in a ponytail, that same raggedy T-shirt that you wear to bed every night, and "the big drawers." For the sake of men all over the world, burn the granny panties. If you're concerned about comfort, there's plenty of sexy and alluring cotton types. Keep it tight and it'll be all right.

Image Is Everything

Be conscious of the type of image you present when you dress. How you dress and how you carry yourself is the blueprint men use to build their strategy for approaching you. Women often observe men breaking their necks in an attempt to check out the women who are provocatively dressed, but that's not always a good thing. It's important for you to understand why a man gives a woman that type of attention. Everyone likes to be noticed, but some attention you can do without. Yes, men can appreciate a woman who is sexily dressed, but there is a distinct difference between sexy classy and sexy trashy. If a man judges that you're dressed sexy trashy, he is almost certain to approach you in a way that's commensurate. On the other hand, if he determines you're dressed with class, more often than not he will approach you with dignity and respect. If you find yourself consistently being approached in a way that's less than flattering, take the time to analyze the image you're sending out.

Because this is a very subjective topic, I decided to informally poll a few men. I asked ten random men, "What's your opinion of women who dress provocatively versus conservatively?" The comments I got were quite interesting. Here are six of the more colorful answers:

1. Dave says, "Hell no. You have no morals if you dress provocatively in public. That's for home."
2. Champagne says, "The ones who dress provocatively are just artificially trying to draw attention to themselves. If I want to get some ass, those are the ones I approach first."
3. Freddie says, "You can be crazy and wild, but leave something to the imagination. Some of the stuff has got to be left just for me."
4. James says, "I like looking at [provocatively dressed women]. I don't want them to be too conservatively dressed, either. I prefer she be with me if she's going to be dressed provocatively."

5. John says, "I don't like provocatively dressed women, mainly because people don't take them seriously."

6. Darryl says, "If a woman is too provocatively dressed, I approach her because she's letting everyone know she might be giving up some ass. She wouldn't be dressed that way if she wanted to keep her good-girl image. I only approach those kinds of women when I want to get some. I'm not trying to have a relationship with them."

Just some food for thought . . .

Men are stingy when it comes to their women dressing provocatively and displaying all the goods. Most men like when their women dress provocatively, but it should be very classy and for them alone. If you're going out with your girlfriends, it is not the time to wear that tight miniskirt with the low-cut top. There's nothing better than another man's woman dressed sexy trashy with her goods exposed to the world. Men like to look, but they'd prefer it not be their woman all the men are drooling over like a centerfold.

Men dread the negatives that accompany being with a woman who's dressed like a hooker. It's inevitably going to put him in a difficult situation. Some brainiac is bound to make a disrespectful comment or do something that is less than tasteful. Then your man is put in a no-win situation. He's going to have to confront the person who made the inappropriate comment, or if he lets it slide, then he's going to have to answer to you. The bottom line is leave something to the imagination.

I've developed a test to help you determine if you're dressed sexy trashy or sexy classy. I had to come up with a way to objectively measure the difference because a lot of women leave the house feeling like, "What man could possibly resist me?" While a better question might be, "What bait are you using to attract him?" Are your nonverbals saying, "Come and get it," or are they saying, "Don't you even think about parting your lips to talk to me"? Here's a quick self-test for you to perform before leaving the house on a date with your man. I would say get a second opinion from one of your girlfriends, but I have noticed time and time again that doesn't necessarily get you very far. Your girl is probably giving off the same vibes you are.

Consider this: Put a hooker on one end of the spectrum—skintight everything, heavy makeup, hair done to the nines, miniskirt barely covering the cat, breasts out, stomach out, and behind out. Now on the other end of the spectrum, let's put together the ultimate image of a prude. How about a librarian type—turtleneck; long, loose-fitting skirt that's mid-shin length; penny loafers; heavy, dark-rimmed glasses; hair pulled back into a nice little bun; and no makeup whatsoever. Now look in the mirror and figure out which side of the spectrum your look is leaning toward. The more characteristics you pull from the hooker side, the greater the chances you're flirting with sexy trashy. Whereas pulling more characteristics from the librarian side leads you to sexy classy. Neither far end of the spectrum is a desirable place to be. Start in the middle, and depending on the circumstance, grab characteristics from one end or the other. If he's introducing you to his mother for the first time, a sheer dress with your nipples doing everything possible to seek daylight is not a classy way to express your sense of fashion. I know you may be saying, "Who would ever do something so ridiculous?" Well, trust me, it's been done before. Always be aware of what image you're conveying.

Pretty is as pretty does. This list is included in case you come across the unfortunate women who live in areas where the positive examples are few. You may be able to help them out. Here are a few areas of which to always be mindful:

1. **Pretty toes.** Men love these. It's an indicator of how meticulous you are about the lesser-seen body parts. You'd be surprised at how many times I've heard men say they couldn't continue a relationship because they couldn't get past all the corns, bunions, onions, and everything else going on with his woman's feet.

2. **Hair.** I know it's difficult to keep that cover girl look every day, but try to do a little something to keep your man's attention. Most men prefer the real thing, and they usually prefer long to short, so if you feel the need for a weave, at least make it believable. Avoid the concrete-like hair gels and the exotic colors (blue, burgundy, and platinum). It's just not very becoming. The natural look almost always beats out the colorful beehive.

3. **Well-manicured hands.** They pretty much have the same impact as well-cared-for toes.

4. **Language.** A woman with a foul mouth is always a turnoff. It's probably best to eliminate cursing from your vocabulary altogether. It's just not very ladylike.

5. **Teeth.** I know I shouldn't have to go into this one, but don't ever let anyone make you believe any color other than white is attractive in your mouth. Gold teeth just aren't cute.

6. **Body odor.** Be mindful of all your smells all the time (breath, skin, pits, feet, and everywhere else). Men talk too. Enough said.

7. **Accessories.** Never overaccessorize. It's a dead give-away that you're trying too hard.

8. **Makeup.** Less is more.

9. **Body hair.** Most men prefer women to be clean shaven or waxed. There are, however, some men who like women with hairy legs. I suggest you seek your man's opinion. If in doubt, opt for hairless.

10. **Body art.** Tattoos are also an enormous turnoff. It makes you look worn. Graffiti isn't even acceptable on a building, so why would you do it to your body?

Nasty habits are another thing you want to get under control if you want to present a polished image to the world. The two big ones that come to mind are smoking and drinking. Smoking is not cool. It's not sexy. It doesn't make you look more mature. It makes you look dumb. You're better off just putting a gun to your head and pulling the trigger. At least you die quickly. Smoking leads you to a slow, painful death. The smell of cigarette smoke infiltrates your clothes, house, car, and just about everything else. Perfume and a whole pack of Tic Tacs can't get rid of the funk that cigarettes leave behind. Smoking is also a dead giveaway of a weak mind. If you're willing to smoke, it makes one question what other things you might be willing to do.

Alcohol needs to be handled with extreme care. Be careful.

What Have You Done for Me Lately?

Thorny point #2. Gold diggers. If you're not familiar with the term, it's a woman (for the purposes of this discussion) who enters into a relationship with the goal of monetary or material gain. Simply put, *gold digger* is a kinder and gentler name for a modern-day prostitute. These women would never describe themselves as prostitutes, though. I assume it's because they don't walk the street, but it is what it is. They come from all walks of life—high school drop-outs to highly educated professionals. What differentiates them from other women is the fact they will only entertain men who have what they see as significant wealth. Wealth is their primary criteria for finding a man.

I often hear women attempt to justify their actions by saying, "Why not? He's getting what he wants, and I'm getting what I want. Why give it away for free?" This is the ultimate form of self-degradation and lack of self-esteem. Remember, you only have one body. If you ever decide to trade or barter something, shouldn't it at least be of equal or greater value? When a woman trades her body for a piece of paper, that's far from an equal trade. Think about it. What are you saying about your self-worth by doing this? Never sell yourself cheap. That's like going to a man and saying, "Hey, mister, I've got a million dollars in this suitcase. If you give me one dollar, I'll give you the million." Now how much sense does that make? None. Remember, it was women's bodies that produced the greatest people on earth. Every king, queen, doctor, and billionaire came from the womb of a woman. Your body is your temple.

Any savvy man can see right through a gold digger's MO. Some men will gladly make the trade because they know it's a lopsided agreement. Others want still more. They want to get you in bed, and still have you pay (through the power of suggestion). And yet, there are plenty of honest, hardworking men looking for a good woman with pure intentions. These are the men who have gone to great lengths to beat these unscrupulous women at their own game. Once a man sniffs out that she may be in it for the money, he will downplay his wealth in order to determine if her interest in him is real. Some affluent men may choose to use some tricks of their own to trip her up:

1. He might take her out on dates and never invite her to his home.
2. He could purposely drive an old beat-up car on a date when he has multiple expensive cars at home.
3. He may intentionally dress down to appear less affluent.

4. If a man has a high-profile occupation, many times he will claim one of his less-impressive hobbies as his full-time job.

5. Some men will even test a woman by giving her what she might perceive to be a large sum of money. His purpose is to see if she would take it and what she chooses to do with it. Will she go shopping and blow it? Will she spend it on him? Will she save or invest it?

When you choose to date an affluent man, it's important that you learn to deal with him honestly and directly, as you should with any man. However, you've got to understand where he's coming from. Affluent men tend to be much more skeptical of a woman's intentions than your average man because they're trying to protect their wealth. There is a difference between you going after a man who is successful, goal oriented, and a strong leader, and him coming after you. This is where old-fashioned values will carry you a long way. The early stages of dating are merely an experiment in negotiation. The better negotiator you are, the better the chances are of you getting what you want. The key to successful negotiating is to always do it from a position of strength. Your greatest strength is not needing what he has to offer. Even if you do need it or desire it, he should believe there isn't enough money in the world to buy your love. Developing the reputation of a gold digger can stick with you for a lifetime. Your dignity and values should never be bought. Let him demonstrate that he knows how to treat a lady, and always remember the list of nevers we discussed earlier in the chapter.

The Video Ho

Thorny point #3. The images the hip-hop music industry pipes into homes all over the world are very destructive to our young women. They portray to the world that women are promiscuous sexual objects. I'm sure the phrase *video ho* is as difficult to read as it is for me to write; however, that label has been placed on the women who appear in many of today's sexually provocative hip-hop videos. I don't condone it, but when you allow yourself to be exploited, you might have to live with some labels that are less than flattering. The booty-shakin', breast-jigglin', pelvis-gyratin', Daisy Dukes–wearin' depiction of our young women is absolutely devastating to our children and our children's children. Our young boys and girls grow up accepting those images as reality. Boys grow up to be men and emulate the degradation of women that has been poured into their heads for as long as they can remember. They actually think it's acceptable and cool to refer to ladies as bitches and hos. What's even worse is the fact that young girls rarely take exception to those labels. They grow up idolizing these exploited women and have dreams of one day being in a video themselves. The madness has got to stop.

Those images of fast cars, fast women, and a luxurious, carefree lifestyle are manufactured. It is not reality. The hip-hop industry uses that form of marketing to sell CDs. The cars are rented, the houses are leased, and the women exploited. They are literally treated as sexual objects. Many of these women stoop to unmentionable depths to experience a world that doesn't really exist. It's all done in the name of money. Don't get caught up.

In the book *Confessions of a Video Vixen*, Karrine Steffans says, "Like so many young girls, I grew up wanting to be famous. I used to watch television and dream about the Beverly Hills lifestyle seen in all my favorite films . . . I reached most of my goals, but I didn't do it in a conventional way. I did it using the oldest trick in the book. Sex . . . The top reason a woman finds herself in a rap video, sprawled undressed over a luxury car while a rapper is saying lewd things about her, is a lack of self-esteem . . . No one who values, loves, or knows herself would allow herself to be placed in such a degrading position."

I want to call attention to the word that she used in the last sentence—*allow*. There's no one who can make you present yourself in a classless manner. The only way it can happen is if you allow it. Remember your power!

STANKONYA

Thorny point #4. Men love women with energy, a smile, a pleasant disposition, and a passion for life. This issue may seem a little pointless to some women, but most men can recount numerous instances when they've come across a woman with a "Stankonya" attitude. The worst part about it is that it's usually unwarranted. You can be the most beautiful woman in the world, but if your attitude stinks to the high heavens, men will distance themselves from you. Inner beauty always outshines external beauty. It's one thing for a woman to play coy, but no one likes a sourpuss. Just because you're having a bad day, it doesn't mean you have the right to drag innocent bystanders down in the pit with you. There are women who won't offer a man a pleasant tone of voice. They won't give him eye contact. They won't even give him the common courtesy of speaking when being spoken to. You should always exude positive energy. Positive people draw others closer, whereas negative people repel them. When a man politely says, "Hi," give him a smile and say, "Hello," back. If you're out dancing, and a man respectfully asks you to dance, either dance, or smile and cordially say, "No, thank you." I can't stand to see a woman just ignore a brother like he doesn't exist. It's rude. What could it possibly cost you to just acknowledge him as a human being? Think about the times you've encountered the eye-rollin', impatient, hand-on-the-hip sister at the cash register asking, "What do you want?" Doesn't that attitude just make the hair stand up on the back of your neck? Even if you're approached in a way that's less than tactful, you should still maintain your values and self-respect. I know it sounds basic, but treat people as you would want to be treated. Working to remove those ugly thorns will allow the world to behold your incredible beauty.

CHAPTER FOUR

KEEPING THE "PIECE"

BY NOW YOU SHOULD KNOW WHAT I MEAN WHEN I SAY *PIECE*. In case you forgot, it's my way of referring to sex. You should also know it's more valuable than gold. It is so highly sought after that men have risked life and limb in order to find just a little piece. They risk their families by cheating for it. They risk their lives by choosing to sleep with women, not knowing whether they have life-threatening diseases like HIV or AIDS. They literally risk their salvation by exercising their free will against God's wishes. And guess who holds the key to the treasure chest that holds the oh-so-valuable piece? You do. That's where the key should remain—with you. Isn't it awesome to know that you alone possess something that's so valuable a man is willing to give up everything he has for it? It's an equally awesome responsibility to protect it and use it responsibly.

I want you to do what millions of teens and adults wish they would have done—be a piece keeper. Just about anyone will tell you if they had to do it all over again, they would have kept the piece. If you don't believe me, find out for yourself. Take an informal poll of as many women as you can find. Ask them, "If you had it to do all over again, would you have remained a virgin until you got married?" I'm willing to bet the great majority of them will tell you emphatically, "Yes." The reasons can vary, but most women don't really value their virginity until they lose it. As a woman, you can equate it to stepping into a jail cell, letting the prisoner out, and giving him the key. For most women, all of your power is now in the hands of someone who doesn't even deserve it.

What's even sadder is that many of the women who are giving it up just don't know any better. Younger women think it's the force that keeps a man, but little do they know it's the very thing that runs him off. Mature women tend to think that if it's the best he ever had, he won't ever choose to be with another woman. Not. These are the same misguided women who can't figure out why they're always involved with a man who just won't commit. They also won't acknowledge that the reason they're an emotional wreck after a failed relationship is not merely because they lost someone they cared for, but even more because they gave away one of the most valuable treasures that exists on the earth—the piece. It's not until they've lived long enough and experienced enough heartache that they realize, "If only

I had waited." I assure you, this chapter will change the tactics you use to get and keep a man. It will help you to find Mr. Right, not just Mr. Right Now. There are a number of complex issues that stem from this subject, but I'll cut right to the chase. If you've already been there and done that, it's never too late to take control and be a piece keeper.

In order to fully understand where I'm coming from, it's important to first analyze why so many women, young and old, choose to give up the piece. The whys can be broken down into three categories: a woman's upbringing, a lack of sufficient knowledge about herself, and her general misunderstanding of men. It's important that you understand the challenges each of these areas present. If you can understand the whys, you will be better prepared to say no and mean it when men approach you for sex. A large number of women don't really understand why they should say no, and it's not until it's too late that they begin to get the picture. My intent is to give you the confidence to say no and a clear understanding of why it's important.

They'll Be What They See

One of the most devastating factors that has driven women to explore sex at an early age is the deterioration of the family unit. Understanding the impact of your upbringing and the environment you're brought up in is critical to being a successful piece keeper. In the majority of single-parent homes, the mother is the primary caregiver. This means that the girls being raised by single mothers have no example of how they are supposed to interact with men. A mother's love can never be matched, but a father's importance should never be underestimated. As we discussed in Chapter 1, a father's love is vital to a girl's development. A father's love should be a girl's first experience with love from a man. This special relationship allows a girl to experience unconditional love without ever being expected to perform sexually. She can hug and kiss her father, she can hold his hand, they can laugh and play together, they can even sit together and do absolutely nothing at all. He's there to provide for and protect her, and he always has her back. Aren't these basically the same things every grown woman ultimately looks for in a man?

Too many people make the mistake of thinking a girl needs her mother more than she needs her father and a boy needs his dad more than he needs his mother. The truth of the matter is that children need both parents equally. One parent can never compensate for the absence of the other. Therefore, the girls who have the misfortune of having only one parent in their lives often have to develop that missing piece of their personality by trial and error. The interesting part is that most women don't even realize their development is incomplete until they're actually in a relationship with a man. They really don't know his physical and emotional needs, and how would they if they didn't have an example? A strong male figure is crucial to a woman's confidence in dating and marriage.

For the women who have loving and caring fathers in their lives, try to imagine how different life would be if your father weren't around as you were growing up. How would you learn the skills of being a wife, or even a girlfriend, if your father wasn't present as a role model? A single mother can only be an example of a good mother. Being a positive role model of how to deal with men is much more difficult if she's not married. Multiple boyfriends just aren't suitable substitutes. However, it's very important for single mothers to understand that their daughters have a great possibility of growing up with less than optimal relationship skills unless a conscious effort is made to get her the information she needs to be successful. Otherwise, children grow up relationship handicapped, and that only leads to bad decision making. As a result, many daughters are forced to learn about relationships from their environment. Let that marinate for a minute or two. Think about how devastating that can be. With all of the negative input children gain from today's society, there's a better chance of them receiving the wrong information than hearing what's right.

Many single mothers feel they are projecting a positive image to their children by not bringing men around, but that's not necessarily true. When a woman finds a strong and stable relationship, her children need to learn from her example. That doesn't mean bringing a different man to the house every week and calling that relationship stable. A child can and must learn from home. The family should be the greatest teacher, otherwise daughters must gain their experiences from a society that can easily steer them in the wrong direction. For example, schools are issuing them condoms. The media is bombarding them with images of irresponsible sex and glorifying ghetto life, baby mamas, and baby daddies. Their friends usually can't offer much guidance because they're often facing many of the same dilemmas. So, where does a young girl truly learn how to have a respectful relationship with a man when so much of what she sees is negative? When would she have the opportunity to learn that love is so much more than sex? Just about never. And the streets are a very unforgiving teacher. Often the cycle then repeats itself generation after generation.

I bring up the disadvantages women from broken homes face in an effort to show why a woman who grows up with this type of social handicap is extremely vulnerable to opportunistic men. It's almost as if she's wearing a neon sign around her neck that says, "I'm looking for love in all the wrong places. Come get a piece while the getting's good." A savvy man can usually spot a woman who grew up without a solid male figure in her life. The secret is in the way she carries herself. When women lack that male figure during their upbringing, they tend to develop a mind-set that they need to be intimate with a man in order to gain his love, to keep him, to satisfy him. They feel that sex is the way to a man's heart. And why wouldn't they? That's what the media presents as the truth; that's the myth that today's society perpetuates. If there's no example at home, then that's their reality. As a result, these are the very women whom men take advantage of. They want you to believe that nonsense. That's why so many women find themselves in a relationship wishing for a commitment and thinking that sex is the key to getting a man. Any man will tell you sex is important, but it is not what ultimately drives him to the altar. This mentality of trading sex for love touches every segment of our society. It's this mind-set that has literally crippled the state of relationships in our country. Love is something you do, not who you do.

A woman usually gives sex in hopes of gaining the bigger prize—the relationship. A man, on the other hand, gives in to a relationship to gain the bigger prize—sex. With such a huge divide in the way men and women think about sex and relationships, it's no wonder we can't seem to sing from the same sheet of music. The same thing applies to marriage. Men get married thinking they can now have sex for breakfast, lunch, and dinner. Women, however, get married thinking, *Whew! I don't have to do my chandelier act anymore*. It's just another one of those fundamental differences in the way men and women are wired. Attempting to exchange sex for love is the furthest you can ever be from the truth. If you don't learn anything else from this book, learn this: Sex may stimulate a man's body, but it does not stimulate his heart. If your body is what you use to catch him, it's going to take that same body to keep him. Think about how easy it is for him to find a replacement. There are nice bodies just about anywhere. A man *must* love more about you than your body, so give him that opportunity by keeping the piece.

For whatever reason, older women often think, *What's the point? I've had sex all of my life, so why change now?* Age makes no difference. If you really want the relationship you've dreamed of, you absolutely, positively, have got to keep the piece until you're married. It's never too late, and I'll tell you why. If you give a man your time, your love, and your body, in his mind, he has absolutely nothing to get married for. Women give men so much power over them during dating that it's ridiculous. If it weren't so sad, it would almost be comical. Let's explore these dynamics as if we were watching through a crystal ball.

Mike is attracted to Beverly and realizes she might be his future wife. Beverly is attracted to Mike and wants to eventually marry him as well. Therefore, Beverly has sex with Mike, cooks for him, is loyal to him, is obedient to him. Mike gladly receives all that is so graciously given. His stomach is full; his woman is loyal, which allows his mind to be content; and his flesh is satisfied because he is getting all of the sex he could ever want. Beverly has relinquished all power to Mike. He now knows Beverly is willing to do whatever is required to keep the relationship moving toward marriage. Mike is now content and very thrilled to have all the power, which he was never entitled to have. Mike knows that if he marries Beverly she will repossess the power that she gave away. That being the case, Mike chooses to hold out from marriage and keep Beverly under his thumb. Beverly is now forever frustrated and confused because she has given Mike everything he could possibly want, but has no true commitment of marriage.

The moral of the story is, if marriage is starting to call and you're giving your man your all, be prepared to take a fall. Some men just don't deserve your very best. Hopefully my crystal ball has allowed you to see that trading a piece for love just doesn't work.

He's Gotta Have It

I often hear women complaining about men wanting to sow their wild oats and not being willing to commit to a relationship. Yes, men do need a certain amount of exploration, but it's not that they don't want to commit, it's more that women don't demand the commitment of marriage before they give up a piece. There are so many women willing to give a man a piece without a commitment that he can't realistically see why he should have to work for it. He also has a difficult time justifying just one piece when there is so much more to be had. Some people call it wanting their cake and eating it too. I equate it to putting a crackhead in the crack house with all he can smoke for free. If you don't make a man commit, he's going to take all he can get. It's not right, and I'm not justifying it. I'm just trying to make you aware that women need to do something different if they want a different outcome.

A man will float from one woman's bed to the next because a woman gives him what he ultimately wants—a piece—before she gets what she ultimately wants—a relationship. That's why she can't keep him. She leaves him no reason to get married. When you give him a piece, he's less motivated to learn about you as a person. He's more motivated to learn about the next sexual rendezvous.

Get yours first. Imagine what would happen if more women took this approach. Our families, our communities, and our country would be more stable. Instead of a woman begging for a commitment from a man as he jumps from one woman's bed to next, the control would be back in the woman's hands. A man would have to learn more monogamous habits. Instead of men sleeping around with multiple women, they'd be more apt to try and build a relationship first. Men would have no choice but to conform. They'd have to learn how to court a woman again. Is that asking too much? I don't think so.

In the 1970s, the country had thousands of people hopelessly addicted to cigarettes and chose to take action. The government developed and pushed a very powerful media campaign to curb the population's appetite for cigarettes. Now, more than thirty years later, smoking has become widely unacceptable in the United States. If we have the ability to decrease the number of smokers and to influence people to ostracize those who still do, we can do the same with casual sex. In today's world, women have been defeated, and defeated badly, because the gender whose priorities are sex first and relationship second is calling the shots. Why should you settle for this when you have the power to make the rules?

The secret here is knowing a man's gotta have it. Understand it, and ingrain it in your mind. As we discussed in Chapter 1, just about everything a man does, he does with sex in mind. Why, you ask? First of all, men are simply wired differently than women. Secondly, they've got to handle their sex-making tool much more often than women do. They've got to whip it out to go to the restroom, they've got to adjust it when they put on their clothes, they've got to look at it and touch it multiple times every day. Also, don't forget, men are visual creatures, and the mere sight of an attractive woman can redirect blood flow from the big head to the little one. Men get sexually aroused much more easily than women.

Take fifteen-year-old boys at a high school dance, for example. Remember how the girls would always complain about the boys not asking them to dance on a slow song?

The girls thought it was because the boys were just shy or trying to be cool, but that's far from the real reason. The real reason is that boys know if a cute little girl rubs against them in the wrong (or right) way, a little "friend" is going to cut in on the dance, and it will be a long and embarrassing walk back to their friends when the song is over. That's why they keep their hands in their pockets. It's not to be cool; it's to keep from looking like a fool. It's almost as if Willy the worm has a mind of its own.

Women, on the other hand, can shut down the "candy store" at will. They can literally set the piece on the shelf and let it collect dust until they decide to go back and use it. How many women do you know who get sexually aroused by a simple dance? Not many. It's not that women don't enjoy sex, they're just wired differently. With the type of control women possess over their sexual desires, there is no reason they can't display the discipline required to hold out and force men to make relationships their number one priority. If that's what men had to do, trust me, they would.

When a woman believes sex is the most valuable asset she brings to a relationship, it puts her in a very awkward position, to say the least. It's not much of an asset if it can be bought on any street corner. You have real assets to offer a man, but if you can't recognize them, a man can't either. That's not a position you want to be in. It's awkward because you can't possibly have a fulfilling relationship if you're no more than a warm, willing body. Men have a real hard time viewing you as a wife unless your actions, not your mouth, display the level of your morals and values. Can you really fault a man for taking a piece and throwing back the rest if you know up front that getting a piece is his priority? You must take responsibility for your own actions.

The Double Standard

A man wants a woman he can respect, but he's often willing to sleep with one he doesn't. Know this: He will most likely never commit to the one who doesn't demand a commitment before she gives him a piece. His logic is this, "If she gives me some after only a date or two, how many other guys has she broken off a piece for?" He doesn't want a woman who has been passed around to so many men she can't even keep count. Men are very sensitive to the possibility their woman has had a busload of different sexual partners. A woman can be forty years old, divorced, with two kids, but in his mind, he likes to think she's a virgin.

Men also don't like to hear all the gory details of her past boyfriends and sexual exploits—even though many will ask. If a man does have the guts to ask, don't kiss and tell. Trust me, you will not hear the end of it. I'm not saying you should be dishonest, but there are certain things a lady needs to keep to herself. Men expect you to accept the fact that they've slept around, but women will carry the label of ho, tramp, or slut when they do. In some countries, women are killed or mutilated if found to be with multiple men. Yes, it's a double standard, but men like to believe their woman has been somewhat preserved just for them. Imagine how simple the conversation with your man will be if you were a piece keeper—you would have nothing to tell. Men like it that way.

When a man truly cares for a woman he will wait and comply with her demands. That's how you know when a man's feelings are genuine. If you make it clear you're not giving him a piece until you're married, and he chooses to stick with you, that's the first step of him expressing how he truly feels about you. Judge a man by his actions first and his words second. That's for starters only, however, because some men truly feel in their hearts that they are irresistible. Even though you've told them no, they will continue to see if they can break you down. *Do not play that game.* If he chooses not to respect your position on intimacy, that should be a sign he doesn't care for you as much as he cares for the kitty. Let him go. After all, what have you lost? Absolutely nothing.

You'll appreciate the discipline and sacrifice you endured when you marry a man with whom you've never had sex. Being a piece keeper allows for a stronger and much more durable relationship, mainly because you give yourself the opportunity to learn what all you have in common instead of focusing just on sex. I personally feel that premarital sex is the biggest reason behind our country's embarrassingly high divorce rate. Sex has a way of clouding your thoughts and judgment. It makes you think you're in love and totally compatible, when in actuality, you're as wrong for each other as a cat and a dog. When a man gives it to you right, you start to see light when there's only dark, blue sky where it's truly gray, and right when it's all wrong. Just wait. Keeping the piece is the best way to determine if you're really in love with a man. It's an even greater test for him. You might already know he's the one for you, but, keeping in mind how much emphasis men put on sex, if he's willing to wait, that's a good sign he's serious.

Some people are more visual learners, so consider the following list comparing the benefits of keeping the piece and giving up a piece.

KEEPING THE PIECE

1. You can date multiple men without being considered a tramp.
2. You maintain control of your life and emotions.
3. You maintain your spiritual covenant.
4. You never have to worry about getting pregnant.
5. You don't have to be concerned about contracting sexually transmitted diseases.

6. You can allow a man to show his true feelings for you and not the false ones that sex produces.

7. You can focus on your personal goals.

8. Men will respect and value you.

9. Your peers will envy you.

10. Your marriage has a better chance of succeeding.

11. You make your parents proud.

12. Your husband will cherish you.

13. You have the ability to make full use of your power.

GIVING UP A PIECE

1. You can satisfy the desires of your flesh.

2. You can find out if you're sexually compatible with a man you're considering marrying.

While you're pondering how there can only be two benefits to giving up a piece, think of how your environment and your upbringing impacts the way you approach sex. Do a little introspection. Take a look at yourself and determine what elements in your personality prevent you from taking control of your sex life. Is it that you lack self-esteem? Are you easily influenced by peer pressure? Do you feel that having sex makes you more of a woman? Whatever the answer,

I'm sure you'll find it's something that's easily overcome. You can't fix destructive behaviors unless you acknowledge them as being destructive and understand why they exist.

Often women lack a general understanding of themselves, and this is a huge reason why many struggle with relationships. They look for a man to make them, to motivate them, or to complete them. In order to have a successful sexless relationship, all of those things must exist prior to meeting a man. You have to know who you are, what it is you want from a man, and what you want from life. Whenever you find yourself looking to a man, as many women do, to define or validate your existence, you're in trouble. Men are most attracted to women whose light of confidence and happiness shines brightest. A man should add to the happiness that already existed inside of you prior to the relationship. He should not have to bring the light for the first time to a dark, hopeless pit. If you don't know yourself, trust me, a man has no chance of knowing you, either. Men are not the intuitive creatures women mistakenly hope they are. That fulfillment has to come from within.

Other examples of poor self-esteem are the number of women who have resigned themselves to "sharing" a man. They are either married to a man they know is cheating or they're single and sleeping with a man they know is married. In some areas of the country, women are displaying levels of desperation never before seen. And there are many women who have chosen to lead single, celibate, and lonely lives because they can't keep an exclusive relationship with a man. There are plenty of eligible, good men, so maybe the problem exists with those women who have chosen to be single. Take a look inside yourself first. The only constant in all of your previously failed relationships is you.

Then there are the women who have just decided to "get theirs," and give the piece freely with no emotional commitment. Most women aren't emotionally capable of doing this, but the numbers who try are steadily increasing. The reason I get from women who live this type of lifestyle is almost always, "Men do it, so why can't I?" That is not the solution. The solution lies in keeping the piece. Women accept these types of lifestyles, not because it's ultimately what they desire, but because it's a way of coping with a situation they feel they have no control over. Women today are fed up, confused, and at a complete loss for answers. But again, I say, women have all the power. It's merely a matter of understanding that it exists and implementing it.

Many of our young women are using sex as a rite of passage. Giving a piece does not make you a woman. Just about any animal can have sex. Just because your friends are doing it and think it's cool doesn't mean you have to jump into their pit of ignorance. You should take the lead and be a positive example of what a woman should be. What allows you to truly transition from adolescence to adulthood is being a piece keeper and learning how to control the power you naturally possess.

No Means No

Women have too many definitions and explanations for the word *no,* and it inevitably gets them in trouble. Never flirt with its meaning because men are guaranteed to test whether you really mean it or not. Women, by nature, are more talkative and less aggressive than men. They also tend to be more compassionate and empathetic. These traits often take over when you're trying to keep men out of your pants. Your more gentle nature will get you into trouble every time. When a man is trying to seduce you, that is not the time to use soft and flowery words. Men respond to straight talk. Get comfortable with looking him right in the eye, no smiling, no joking, and firmly tell him, "No."

The real problem shows up when your nonverbals don't match your verbals. To put it simply so you don't mess this one up, don't say *no* but mean *yes.* It seems simple, but let me give you a few examples so you don't miss this point.

Things not to say

1. "No. Don't do that, because you're making my body tingle and I'm about to . . ."

(continued)

2. "No. Stop rubbing my right nipple like that . . . but I didn't say anything about this left one."

3. "No. Don't kiss my ear. I'd rather you kiss my . . ."

Never use the word *no* unless you sincerely mean it. When a man hears that word, it should trigger something in his brain to immediately and definitely stop whatever he's doing. It's very important you learn to use the unaccompanied word *no.* Not, "No, but . . ." You only need to say, "No." When it comes to keeping the piece, there's no time for sparing a man's feelings. Say what you mean, and mean exactly what you say.

Let me add one more word of caution. Women should never use sex as a carrot to motivate men to do right. Bad idea. All you're doing is devaluing yourself. If you choose to give a man some before he has made a commitment, you've already given him motivation to do wrong. The piece should never be used as a bargaining chip. Some women give a man a piece in order to gain something else. That "something else" can come in the form of a commitment, preferential treatment, material goods, or the hope that it will make him act right or that he will verbally express his love for you. It doesn't work. Temporarily, maybe, but is your body really worth bartering? Entirely too many women make the mistake of thinking what they are sharing is so special that their mate will put equal value on it. Don't count on it. In his mind, he's giving you no more than you're giving him. By now you should know that's not the case. The piece is much more valuable, so don't be surprised if he moves on to another woman with complete disregard for the intimate moments you shared in bed.

Silly Man Tricks

As you continue the lifelong process of broadening your knowledge of men, always keep in mind that men spend inordinate amounts of time trying to figure out ways to get around the power of a woman. The better you understand them and why they do the things they do, the more effective you'll be in keeping the piece. As a man matures he picks up new tactics and stores them in his bag of tricks, all in an effort to get you into bed. Don't let age fool you. There are plenty of youngsters out there who are masterful in their ways, while there are also plenty of mature men who possess elementary macking capabilities. The only measly power men possess is concocting schemes to get what they want. Here are a few more silly man tricks I want you to be aware of.

1. A man might prey on a woman's desire to have a family. This one tends to confuse women who are accustomed to giving a free piece every now and then to win a man. If a man attempts to persuade you by talking about someday wanting children, don't read into what he's saying by assuming he's talking about marrying

you. He may want to have children, yes, but you may be nowhere in the picture. That's why we have all these baby mommas today. Many a woman has fallen for the pipe dream of marriage and family just because some man told her he wanted her to have his baby. A man will attempt to play on your nurturing nature by making you believe he's going to marry you or love you more after you have his child. You probably can't even imagine a woman going for this type of approach, but it happens every day. Some women are so desperate they believe whatever they're told. For some men, marriage is not a prerequisite to having children. Do not, do not, do not fall for this age-old nonsense. If he's not doing everything he can to get you to marry him, then getting pregnant brings you no closer to his heart. With that being said, accepting a man's proposal of marriage just because you got pregnant is truly like jumping out of the frying pan and into the fire. It only makes a bad situation worse. A good friend of mine would always say, "Who needs a sperm donor?" There's no honor in being just a baby momma. If you're determined to have children, be equally determined to be a wife. A baby needs a mama and a daddy in the same household.

2. A man will basically tell you directly when he's considering you as the flavor of the month. All you have to

do is listen. If a man asks you out on a date and subsequently says he's not interested in a relationship, tell him to keep on walkin'. Ask him what his purpose is in asking you out if he's not interested in a relationship. Pay close attention to the answer you get because he's really telling you he just wants to have sex. You don't need more friends or people to kick it with, so why fall for that lame excuse? Why would you need a so-called friend who's trying to get in your pants? The *Compact Oxford English Dictionary* defines a friend as, "a person with whom one has a bond of mutual affection, typically one exclusive of sex or family relations." But today the word *friend* can have a variety of meanings. It could be the man you're having sex with, the man you used to have sex with, or the man you tried to have sex with, but for whatever reason decided to leave it alone. Male "friends" are not men with whom you should have intimate relationships. You were doing fine before you met the joker, so keep it moving. These days the word *friend* allows access to "goods" and luxuries that were never given in the past. As long as women continue to give their "friends" a piece, they will be content with maintaining nothing more than a friendship. Women have created this monster too, and now it's going to take women to destroy it. As long as you continue to bring the piece and place it in his lap without demanding accountability and responsibility, he will not hunt for it. If you don't respect your own body, why would you expect him to?

3. Some men try to manipulate you into sex by telling you they love you. Using the "L" word is usually a tactic of last resort. Men who just want to get you into bed will usually try all of the other tricks in their bag before they actually use this one. Men who merely have sex in mind when approaching you know that using the "L" word can get them caught up in a mess of global proportions. Therefore, they try to eliminate that word from their vocabulary completely. But some men will stop at nothing to get their hand in the "cookie jar."

   The words *I love you* can send some women into an uncontrollable tailspin. Since a woman typically values the relationship more than sex, hearing those words may drive many of them into doing things they normally wouldn't do, including giving up a piece. The reason they do it is because they feel they've found the one. But not so fast, my pretty. Men know this is one of the best ways to get through your defenses, and when you let them in you're setting yourself up for the biggest heartbreak known to mankind. *Don't do it.* A savvy man knows an earth-shattering heartbreak for a woman can be hazardous to his health. That is why he uses that tactic as a last resort. A man's actions will display the depth of his love.

He may even try to flip the script by playing your love for him in his favor. Some men will go so far as to say, "If you love me, then show me." Your response should mirror his statement, "If you really love me, then wait." Giving him a piece is not the way to express your feelings. Show your love by having his back, being there during tough times, teaching him, encouraging him, but never feeding into his sexual desires. If a man is genuine in his approach, he will be happy to do just about anything to stay in your good graces.

4. A savvy man understands a woman's body, and he prides himself on finding the areas that drive you crazy, then he exploits them. Most women prefer a man who is sexually experienced over one they have to teach, but if you're a piece keeper, you must work extra hard to keep an experienced man corralled. He knows if he can heat you up, there's a good chance you will reach the point of no return. He will push your sexual boundaries a little bit at a time. This tactic is all about moving slowly so you're not offended, as he sneaks up on the cat. Rapper 50 Cent even has a song called "Just a Lil Bit" that almost describes this approach perfectly. The man will first make what seems like harmless advances—maybe a hug or a kiss. His next objective is to see how far he can go before you stop him. Maybe then he decides to put his hand

on your knee, then your thigh, then farther. Maybe he decides to kiss you on your lips, your neck, and then your breasts. He will continue to explore until you firmly and forcefully let him know you know that game and don't intend to fall for it. Men are persistent, so be aware of what's next. If you won't let him touch you, then he might try the back door. "Well, I won't touch you. Let me just look. Unzip your pants, just a lil bit." *Don't do it.* Remember, his objective is to get you so worked up and horny you will be begging him to take a piece. Many women have taken the fall right here. They think they can handle a little sexual play without actually having sex, and the next thing they know, he's lying in bed next to you smoking a cigar. Why fall for the okie doke? Again I say, men respond best to direct and forceful communication. Don't be subtle about it. You can't be half yes and half no. Your response must be simply "No."

5. One of the most classic ways a man can control a woman is by telling her he wants to get married, but not until he gets his life in order. Some may say they want to wait until they get a job, until their settlement comes in, or until they finish school. In the end, it all means the same thing: He wants to have the milk without buying the cow. There's nothing wrong with having a long-term relationship on your terms, but don't let a

man string you along. As long as you keep the piece, the relationship will be on your terms. If a man is telling you he wants to marry you, and you want to marry him, why can't the joker get his life in order with you as a wife? A good woman should empower her man and make him better, right? Well, let me tell you why he wants to wait. Men use this excuse to buy time. It's also a way for him to keep you pacified until he is through hoin'. If you're not familiar with this term, it basically means he still wants to see other women while keeping you on the hook. His rationale is he doesn't want to cheat on you after you're married, so he'd rather just do it now without the formality of marriage. Don't fall for it. Never let a man use up your valuable years. Being faithful to a woman isn't something that just happens overnight for the cheating types. If a man has cheated on every woman he has ever been with, chances are, marriage is not going to cure him. A man must practice being faithful. While he's dating you is a great time for him to perfect the skill.

Time is one of your most valuable assets—second to the piece, of course—and you must be very conscious not to let a man waste it. Set a realistic mental time frame for yourself to have a formal commitment. Notice I said *realistic* time frame. Pressuring a man toward marriage when you haven't even dated a year is a bit much, in my opinion. However, once he passes your limit, you've got to be proactive and take matters into your own hands. You have to start limiting your time with him. Stop being fully accessible. Find other ways to spend your time. Do things with your friends. Don't immediately start seeing other men because then he'll think you're the one who's no good, but it's important for you to start to wean yourself off him. When he notices a change in your behavior, tell him with compassion, empathy, and caring what it is you expect from him. Don't make any idle threats. Say what you mean, and mean what you say. Any man who truly cares about you will step up to the plate. If that doesn't light a fire under him, he didn't really care about you anyway. Ultimatums are where most women stumble in trying to get their man to act. You should never attempt to bully a man into a commitment. Remember, actions speak a heck of a lot louder than words. Men are accustomed to women talking a lot, but they're not used to them acting first and talking second.

Why Men Lie

For some odd reason I felt compelled to include this section right after Silly Man Tricks. I know it sounds like a very loaded topic, but I'll just touch on the highlights that deal with dating and relationships. The reason men lie seems to be fairly simple to me, but women from all over continue to be baffled by men's less-than-truthful moments. Lying is a product of immaturity and lack of experience in dealing with women. Men who are habitual liars just haven't figured out that telling the brutal truth will get them much further than lying ever could. The liars shouldn't be your ultimate concern; they tend to eliminate themselves. You just have to be smart enough to recognize the pattern of lies and handle it swiftly and firmly. The foundation of any healthy relationship is trust, and if you can't trust him, send him on his way. Men who are honest and forthright require more of your concentrated attention, mainly because those are the men with whom women seem to let down their guard. Remember, an honest man can still be very wrong for you.

As to why men lie, I group the lying types into two categories: those trying to get in and those trying to get out. Those trying to get in rely on lying primarily because they've found it's effective in breaking through a woman's defenses. Keep in mind, most men have been devising ways to circumvent a woman's authority for as long as they can remember. In a nutshell, some men lie because they feel they have to.

Then you have the men who lie in order to get out of a relationship. This usually occurs when men try to avoid a woman's emotional meltdown that results from a failed relationship. The crocodile tears, yelling, screaming, and piercing looks of disgust and disappointment are never a man's idea of fun. Therefore, they tend to say whatever they have to in order to minimize the blow to her feelings. That's his way of trying not to hurt her too much.

THE DATING CATCH-22

The dating catch-22 is where tests and temptation start to take a toll on your mind and body. If you're not familiar with the term *catch-22*, it's defined by the *American Heritage Dictionary of the English Language*, as "a situation in which a desired outcome or solution is impossible to attain because of a set of inherently illogical rules or conditions." Simply put, it's a "damned if you do, damned if you don't" situation. Ultimately, the desired outcome is to keep the piece until you find a man you love and one who loves you back—your husband. However, the situations that present themselves between the time you make your vow to keep the piece and your wedding vows can sometimes make your goal seem unattainable—unless you have a plan. Knowledge is power, right? Attempt to learn and understand the things that can potentially derail your efforts to keep the piece. That way you gain power over them.

Often women start off with the greatest of intentions. They make vows to their family, society, the church, and even God that they will keep the piece until they are married, but just as determined as you are to keep it, others are equally determined to see that you don't. There are also times your mind plays tricks on you and you begin to wonder if you're really doing the right thing. That is why it's so important to truly know yourself, your body, your mind, your capabilities, and your limits. You will be tested and tempted time and time again. You've got to stick to your guns. I know you can do it.

Here is the first piece of the catch-22 dilemma. When you have no man in your life and you're keeping the piece, everything is fine and good, right? Well, I've met many women who see this as the problem. They don't want to be alone. Isn't the whole point of preserving yourself to attract and keep the right man? Most women desire to have that special man in their lives, but not having one for long periods can play tricks on your mind. You begin to doubt if what you're doing is truly the best thing. Your girlfriends tell you about what they did with their boyfriends. You fantasize about what it would be like to do it. Your patience wears thin after a while. Just about any similarly shaped object resembling a certain portion of the male anatomy sends your body temperature through the roof. Your flesh screams for fulfillment. The pressure pushes some women to literally take matters into their own hands, or potentially deal with the wrong man because they feel they're about to burst.

To remedy this situation you figure it's probably best to do more dating in an effort to find Mr. Right. That brings me to the first critical part of the dating catch-22. I believe it's very important to expose yourself to more men by dating, but pay attention as I set the stage. There is absolutely nothing wrong with dating different men. It's healthy because it opens your eyes to the different types of men out there. It's very hard to determine what kind of man you desire when you really haven't dated enough to know your preferences. Dating can help in narrowing down the different flavors of men. Don't be discouraged by all of the less-than-flattering names people call women who date multiple men. Those don't apply to you when you're a piece keeper. Dating should be enjoyable. After all, you have all the power, you set the rules, and you can freely move from one guy to the next because the only thing you've invested is time. It's the women who give up the piece to every man they date who get labeled with those unflattering names. Those are also the same women who experience an emotional train wreck when the relationship doesn't work out. You won't have that problem, because you're keeping the piece under lock and key. But it's important to understand that greater exposure to men through dating is where the tests and temptations begin.

Here's a helpful tip when dating multiple men: Always be honest and up front. Let them know they aren't the only one you're dating. The goal is to find out sooner rather than later if the guy you're dating is garbage. The more you can learn from a man up front, the better off you'll be. It's easy to get involved with a nut, but hard to get out. In the end, it will be your honesty and willingness to move on that will have men jumping through hoops to win your love. Men want what they can't have, and they want what everyone else wants as well. It's human nature. Giving the impression he isn't the greatest thing since sliced bread makes him want you more. If you're too needy initially, he will think you're desperate and have no other options.

Dating a variety of men also gives you the benefit of fine-tuning the list of characteristics that are important to you in a husband. Men come in all shapes, sizes, and colors. Take your time. Find the type that's right for you. How do you really know what you like if you don't date different men? This is an area that drives men crazy because women say they want one thing, but they really want another. Many times they have no idea what they want and why. You might find the successful entrepreneur you thought you wanted has a very limited amount of quality time to spend with you. The extra-fine pretty boy with the wavy hair and muscles may sound like Mr. Right, but the other twenty women he's seeing might think so as well. Date different men before you settle down with just one. It will give you the confidence when you get married that you made the right decision.

If your impatience gets the best of you, you will settle and find a man who's not Mr. Right, but Mr. Right Now. You think he's nice, but you know he's not the man you intend to marry. One thing leads to another, and you decide to go ahead and break him off a piece. Now, for what it's worth, you're a part of the in crowd. Instead of being a special rare find, you've jumped in the pot with all the other desperate women. Mr. Right Now has become the person with whom you spend all of your time because you shared your treasure with him. You don't want to leave because you've given something so special. Mr. Right can't find you because Mr. Right Now is taking up all of your quality time. The other problem is Mr. Right Now has no plans of moving on to someone else because he is completely content with the way things are. He's getting exactly what he wants. This is obviously not your desired result.

Part two of the dating catch-22 dilemma is where it becomes important to be familiar with who you are as a woman. Being around a man to whom you're attracted causes your mind and body to do even more strange things. Let's say you found a really nice guy you would like to get to know better. You go on a few dates and fireworks start to fly. As things continue to heat up between the two of you, you take the time to inform him you're a piece keeper. You should always make it a point to proudly tell him you're not interested in having sex until you are married. It's cruel and unusual punishment to lead a man to think he's going to get some, then you put on the brakes out of nowhere. This conversation will weed out a lot of men who were approaching you because they thought that they might get a piece. This guy chooses to stay because he thinks he can wait you out. In his mind, he knows he can break you down.

You think you've found Mr. Right. He is everything that you imagined. Unfortunately, he can also sense that you're really feeling him, and he knows you're tangled in his web of love. Most men respect the fact that a woman wants to keep the piece and will go along with the program—to a point. Here's the rub. Now you're a challenge. He wants what he can't have, but he's not willing to quit just yet. Your Mr. Right decides to keep you because he knows you're a good girl, but while he's waiting for you to come around, he decides to find a different woman who will give him a piece. In his mind, he thinks he's doing the right thing because you're the one he cares about and this other woman was just something to do. What is going on? First you found a buster you couldn't get rid of because you gave him some, and now you've found what appears to be Mr. Right who's cheating because you didn't give him some. This isn't fair, but it's something that happens every day. It's inexcusable, but I felt it was important for you to be aware of. It's a dating catch-22. Finding a man with character and integrity should be first on your list.

Keep the piece.

CHAPTER FIVE

Give Him a "Peace"

"It is better to live in a corner of the roof than in a house shared with a contentious woman."

—PROVERBS 25:24

I THOUGHT THIS QUOTE WOULD HELP ME TO EXPLAIN HOW crucial it is to give your man peace in his life. First, let's study the word *contentious* as defined by *The Oxford Pocket Dictionary of Current English.* It means "causing or likely to cause an argument." There are some other words that are synonymous that really drive home the meaning, like *belligerent, combatant, quarrelsome, fierce, vehement, argumentative,* and *disagreeable.* These are all words that describe the type of woman who drives men to the rooftop. It was obviously written to remind women of how difficult they can be at times because there can't be a man alive who doesn't already know how unbearable women can be. Women must understand there is no room in a relationship for a contentious spirit. I feel this scripture acknowledges the fact that women have all the power to make the home a happy place or one where even the most evil dare not enter. I say that tongue in cheek. But all jokes aside, if you want your relationship to last, you've got to constantly remind yourself that a man's peace is the foundation of his happiness. It takes two to argue and fight, so why not take the high road?

Consider the number of times you've seen couples reach a complete deadlock in a disagreement; he's not speaking to her because his needs aren't being met, and she's not speaking to him because her needs aren't being met. Someone has got to be the first to give in. Don't be too proud to be the first to offer the "peace pipe." Since you have the most power in the relationship, you also have the greater responsibility to promote and sustain peace. It's very similar to a parent-child relationship. If you get angry with your child because he was acting up, you don't sit around and wait for him to apologize before you talk to him again. You are the parent, so you carry the greater responsibility to explain why you did what you did and to make things right.

Black women in the United States have developed a reputation for being contentious—whether it's justified or not is a whole different book. I personally think black women have been forced to assume the position of matriarch in their families due to a number of socioeconomic issues that have blotted America's history since its inception. Often black women have a difficult time releasing that position to the men they love. They also tend to teach their daughters to possess the same type of strength, which inevitably causes conflict. Whenever there are two strong leaders vying for the same space, a fight ensues—contention. Don't allow yourself to get caught up in this type of destructive thinking. A real man who is a leader should never have to compete with you for position in the family. This, in part, is another reason why we have so many single-parent families.

It's very difficult for a man to lead and be attentive to your needs when he's preoccupied with trying to maintain his sanity. I wish some women could have an out-of-body experience to see and hear how they come across to the man they care about. I think they would understand why men fight so hard not to be consumed by the attacks on their peace of mind. In order to get the most mileage out of your man, you should never underestimate the importance of giving him peace. That means minimizing conflict, practicing communication without provocation, and learning the secrets that win a man's loyalty. If you're dating and intend to make it to the altar with the right man, or even if your goal is merely to have a special relationship, this is the best way to make him feel loved without having to use your body.

These days so many women are hung up on what a man can do for them that they rarely consider what they're able to offer him. Try peace. I think you'll be pleasantly surprised with the results. Men cherish women who know how to choose their battles. Life is entirely too short to spend excessive amounts of time arguing over things that aren't really important. Try not to overload him with every little issue you have with him throughout any given day. Some things just aren't significant enough to expend time and energy on. It's okay to discuss the issues about which you're passionate, but some things you've got to live with. When he comes home, give him time to unwind before hitting him with the drama of your day. Men have a way of glazing over when women complain and nag regularly. It makes it difficult to sort the important stuff from the nonsense. He can appreciate a woman who stands up for what she believes in. He can even understand the occasional blowups when she feels she's been done wrong. Most men would rather cross the Sahara Desert with a teaspoon of water before dealing with a contentious woman—or as the Bible suggests, living in a corner of the roof might even be better.

MINIMIZING CONFLICT

This is a concept some women have an extremely hard time comprehending from a man's perspective, but I'm going to make a strong attempt to bring some clarity to it. In a nutshell, most men just want to be left alone. They don't need you constantly being on their backs about every little thing. And men don't want to be changed, or fixed up like an old car, either. Most men feel they are pretty decent as they are, and that's good enough. When a woman makes constant attempts to change her man, or repetitively voices her displeasure, he interprets it as him not being acceptable to her. If she were satisfied, then there would be nothing to complain about, right? Well, that's how he sees it anyhow.

I hate to sound repetitive, but men are simple creatures. They operate more by instinct than women do—yes, almost like a common animal, if that helps you to understand. As much as I hate to say it, they're almost like puppies. (*Dog* is just so cliché.) For example, if you feed a puppy, play ball with him, rub his belly, pat him on the head, talk lovingly to him, and show him the smallest degree of love, he will be your buddy for life. You can open the gate and he'll stay without ever running away because he appreciates your goodness. However, if every time you walk out to the backyard you scream at him, beat him, and consistently show your displeasure, he will run away and find a new home at the first opportunity.

Have you ever noticed how a mistreated puppy lowers his head and scurries along the ground in fear at the very sight of his owner? He'll hide in a corner and wait to see what type of mood is in the air because he doesn't want to get hit or yelled at. However, if his owner calls him with a gentle voice, he'll skeptically peek his head out and make a halfhearted effort to obey, testing to see if all this sweetness is for real. But if the owner raises his hand too fast to scratch his own head, the puppy scurries back to his hiding place in fear of being beaten again. That's because he's accustomed to getting mistreated. Even when the owner decides to be nice and rubs the puppy's belly, he'll accept it, but he's really not feeling the love.

Men are very much the same way. As a matter of fact, if you treated your man the same as you would a puppy, you'd probably get better results. Try talking to him gently, feeding him, playing with him, and rubbing his head and stomach regularly, and watch what happens. He'll give you his heart. The key is to provide a loving and caring environment. You can thank me later for that simple yet powerful piece of insight.

MANAGING YOUR EXPECTATIONS

Women often have unrealistic expectations of a man, which leads to disappointment and dissatisfaction. Many women tend to think a man is going to solve their emotional problems and make them happy. But you are the designer of your own happiness. A man can never make you happy. He can add to your happiness, or possibly even take away from it, but happiness in your relationship starts with a happy you. Some women think a man will make their life better; he'll lift them out of despair and whisk them off to a faraway land. Stop believing that old tale of the knight in shining armor riding in on a white horse to save you. If you expect him to ride in on a mule, it leaves him plenty of room to meet your expectations. Unrealistic expectations set you up for failure. Focus on the things that really matter, like honesty, work ethic, spirituality, or being family oriented. Those types of features carry much more promise.

Many times conflict arises out of unrealistic expectations because the man you have isn't quite the man of your dreams. He isn't six feet five inches and driving a fancy car, writing you poetry every day, and doing everything you tell him to do. The unfortunate truth is reality itself. No man will ever meet all of your preconceived qualities, but there are plenty who can meet the qualities that matter. The man you have may be the perfect one for you, so don't allow yourself to be blinded by the man you imagine or the one your friends and family will think is hot. That will force you to complain, nag, and pick him apart in an attempt to make him fit the mold of the fictitious character in your mind. Nothing drives a man to drink faster than a woman who is never satisfied.

The sad part is that you are the one who causes your own stress and despair. A man can't force you to be with him—you choose him. Why destroy a man's peace by trying to force that square peg into a round hole? He isn't the one at fault; he is who he is. You're at fault for choosing the wrong man. There's no rush. Your man is out there; wait until you find him. You have the power. When you find a man you can give a peace to, you know that you've got the right one. He will sense your satisfaction by the fact that you accept him for who he is, and you're not attempting to change him.

This leads me to another source of misery and faulty expectations women tend to bring on themselves: soul mates. Some women will go through life searching for that one person who is just for them. Out of all the billions of people in the world, does it sound reasonable to believe that there is only one person who can be your soul mate? I don't think so. That sounds like a massive mismanagement of expectations to me. I don't believe in soul mates. I believe there are many people throughout the world who you can consider your perfect match. Your challenge is simply to find one of the many. Managing this expectation will help you not to be too critical with the men you date.

Baggage

This is another huge source of relationship strife. If a woman doesn't have peace and closure from past, failed relationships, how can she possibly bring peace to her new man's life? We have all encountered jerks at some time in our lives, and we all have had some form of tribulation we'd like to forget, but some women have a way of making her "next" pay for the dirt of her ex. Just because your ex cheated doesn't mean your next will. Just because your ex was abusive doesn't mean your next will be. It's nearly impossible to forget events that hurt you to the core, but that shouldn't be your intent. Go ahead and remember that event. Remember what it felt like, but look at it critically and figure out the lessons you learned from it. After you've extracted the lessons, move on and chalk it up to experience.

I like to say that when it comes to relationships you're entitled to one small carry-on. That means all the other major baggage has to be checked at the ticket counter, never to be reclaimed again. You cannot carry that bitterness into relationship after relationship. You never know when the perfect man for you is going to show up. Wouldn't it be a tragedy to let your failed relationship with Mr. Wrong ruin your relationship with Mr. Right?

Sidelined by Your Emotions

Believe it or not, simply mentioning the state of your emotions to a man introduces conflict. Mainly because most people—men or women—can't give you a solid definition of exactly what emotions are. They're subjective and vary greatly from person to person. The problem comes in when women make statements like "You're not meeting my emotional needs" or "I need you to be more sensitive to my emotions." What does that mean? Trying to explain emotions to a man is like trying to teach your cat calculus. When women talk about their emotional needs, it's usually done with such passion and intensity that the only thing men can do is nod and hope to figure it out later. It's extremely difficult to fix something when you have no idea what it is that you're fixing.

Remember, men work most efficiently when logic is involved. The more logical and systematic you are when dealing with conflict in a relationship, the more successful you'll be in finding a peaceful resolution. Emotions are ambiguous and go against the principles of logic. If you hear yourself mentioning the word *emotions* to your man, chances are, he doesn't have the slightest idea how to help you. Try this: When you're having emotional problems with your man or he's not fulfilling you emotionally, sit down and ask yourself, "Self, what exactly is the problem?" Get a piece of paper and actually write down exactly what "self" tells you. Now, sit down with your man and talk about what you have written down. This way you'll be able to get something productive out of him. Men need a direct, concise, and concrete path to your fulfillment. Give him something with which he can work. This reminds me of a story told to me by a friend.

> Wilson and Pam were dating for four months or so. They had what Wilson thought was a pleasant, non-committed relationship. They would talk on the phone, go see movies, and go out to dinner from time to time. They were also intimately involved. During the time they were dating Pam would routinely give Wilson a piece. They both

were professionals and led very busy lives, which meant that they didn't see each other every day. Sometimes several days would go by without them seeing each other. Everything was just peachy until one particular weekend. On Thursday night Pam gave Wilson a piece, and he put it on her like never before—wall-shakin', toe-curlin', headboard-knockin', puttin' it down. Early Friday morning Wilson went out of the country on business and didn't return until Monday. He called Pam once over the weekend and she didn't answer, and he chose not to leave a voice mail. He returned home on Monday and gave her a call to see if they could get together, and Pam was absolutely livid because Wilson didn't call for three days after she had given him a piece. She had a serious Stankonya attitude and loudly repeated to him over and over that he was not sensitive to her emotional needs. Wilson tried to salvage the relationship, although he was confused and utterly amazed that she was making such a big deal over something he saw as so insignificant. In the end, they stopped seeing each other, and to this day Wilson continues to wonder if she was "the one," and the phrase "You're just not sensitive to my emotional needs" continues to ring in his head.

The morals of this story are:

1. Keep the piece. Chances are, if Pam had kept the piece she wouldn't have gotten hurt.

2. Manage your expectations. Pam had given Wilson a piece without a solid commitment. She shouldn't have expected him to call.

3. Avoid ambiguous descriptions of your hurt. Pam could have been much clearer in describing what was irritating her. If she was able to articulate exactly what she was feeling, perhaps Wilson would have understood what she wanted and she would have found out if he was capable of giving that to her.

Don't let your emotions hinder your ability to communicate. You can't get what you want and need if you don't clearly communicate your desires.

Nag No More

"A gentle answer turns away wrath, but a harsh word stirs up anger."

—**PROVERBS 15:1**

Again I must turn to the Bible to help me convey the importance of gentle communication. Regardless of where you come from, whether you're a type A or type B personality, or if you're just having a bad day, harsh words get you nowhere in a relationship. Men are physically stronger, but a woman's tongue balances the playing field. It's important for you to recall that men have a much more aggressive nature than women, and your mouth can get you into some very undesirable situations. Men have shown throughout history that if they can't solve a situation by discussing it, they can resort to brute force. Use your tongue responsibly, and be cautious not to provoke physical aggression.

Some women have a way of unknowingly sabotaging relationships by not understanding how to effectively communicate with their man. One of the main culprits is talking too much. You can't communicate with your man as you would with one of your girlfriends. Men respond to direct and concise talk. Women are much more loquacious, and talking is actually therapeutic to them. Men, on the other hand, prefer fewer words. The more words you use, the greater the chance of him missing out on what it is you're ultimately trying to say. Men like for you to get right to the point—jump through the bush instead of beating around it.

Women often complain that when they're trying to get through to their man, it seems as if they're speaking an entirely different language. The truth of the matter is that in many ways they are. When the words leave your mouth, you intend for them to have one meaning, but by the time they reach his ears, they are interpreted totally differently. For example, if you're the type of woman who consistently and repetitively reminds, suggests, proposes, or recommends things to your man, it's important to know he may choose to describe your actions quite differently. Words like *complaining, nagging, unhappy,* or *dissatisfied* are often more accurate to him. If you're a woman who likes to discuss, confer, or talk through things, your man might see it more as an argument, a debate, or a dispute. I also feel it necessary to remind you that men don't like to be given instructions unless they ask for them. When you offer, it's often construed as you seeing him as not being capable. Women, however, take it as an insult if you don't offer assistance or instruction before she has to ask. Learning these subtle differences will save you a lot of grief when communicating with your man.

PRAISE!

One way you can overcome this communication gap is by practicing the praise technique. This approach was made famous by the legendary boxing trainer and Hall of Fame inductee Angelo Dundee. He trained Muhammad Ali at the peak of his career and was able to motivate him to do some absolutely remarkable things. Women tend to make a fuss over having to cater to man's ego. Well, such is life. There is arguably no ego greater than that of Muhammad Ali. If Angelo was able to communicate with him and get a favorable response, imagine what you can do with your man by using the same technique.

Women scream, yell, pout, mope, nag, and do just about anything else you can imagine to get their men to listen. None of that is necessary. Instead of fighting against his ego, use it to your benefit. If you can't beat 'em, join 'em, just like Angelo did.

Here's what you have to do: Find one of the things your man does that just drives you crazy. There may be many, but try to focus on one for now. Let's start with something simple. For instance, maybe he often forgets to put the toilet seat down when he's finished using the restroom. Subsequently, you're the one who ends up falling in. Most women would nag their man to death in hopes that one day he would develop a habit of peeing and then placing the seat down. Your man gets tired of hearing it, and you get tired of saying it. So instead try this: The next time you're among friends and he's within earshot of the conversation, praise him by telling your friends how wonderful he is about putting the toilet seat down. When you're among family, tell them how good he is about putting the seat down, and the next time you go into the restroom after him, say something to him like, "Thank God I don't have to worry about putting the seat down every time like Tonya [pick a friend's name] does." Eventually your man will believe he is the best seat raiser and returner ever. You have just fed his ego and modified his behavior without ever screaming.

Try it for yourself. It works wonderfully. Just identify

the behavior you want to change and praise him as if it were already changed. If he leaves his underwear on the floor, praise it away. If he doesn't open the car door for you, just praise it away. Even if he doesn't like to take a bath, praise will do the trick. This is a fabulous way to give your man peace, change his behavior, and have him love you even more for being so positive and supportive. The great part is he'll actually begin to think he did it all by himself.

Let Your Feet Do the Talking

Another less confrontational technique you can use to modify your man's behavior is to remember the old saying "Actions speak louder than words." Talk is cheap, and with men it's even cheaper. Women are masterful at talking about what they would do if their man did this or if their man did that. Men know they have quite a bit of leeway before a woman actually does what she says she's going to do, so a savvy man will push the limits to see just how much he can get away with. He also knows a woman will bend and bend some more. What he tends to forget is when she's had enough, she has truly had enough.

Now, your goal in this technique is to condition the men you date to realize you mean what you say and say what you mean. It's impossible to get them to learn that lesson if you continue to simply talk about what you're gonna do. You've got to take action. Stop moving your lips, and move your feet instead. Modification requires minimal confrontation. Why badger him about not taking you out for dinner and a nice evening on the town when you can go yourself? Why nag him to buy you nice jewelry? Buy it yourself. If the grass needs to be cut, and you've asked him one too many times, hire someone to cut it. Men expect you to wait on them and depend on them, but when you choose to take matters into your own hands, it will force us to spring into action. No one likes game playing, but it's important to understand human nature. No one likes a nagging complainer, either. This is merely another method that hits a man where it hurts—right in the middle of his ego.

Winning His Loyalty

There are women who are liked, there are women who are loved, and then there are women who are cherished. You want to be the woman who is cherished. She is hard to find in this day and age, only because many women are more concerned about their own needs and not willing to dive deeply into the desires of their man. In order to hold that coveted position in a man's life, you must internalize the things I've been teaching you, and you have to actively seek out the people, places, and things your man holds dear to his heart. Once you discover what those things are, see to it your relationship doesn't permanently interfere with them. This includes putting your own needs second from time to time, in order to ensure he's able to do some of the things that are special to him. Those moments to him are priceless.

I'm not talking about just any old wants. I'm talking about the things he really treasures. Let me make one thing perfectly clear: This technique must be used only after you get yours. You need to allow plenty of opportunity for him to pursue you. Let him show his commitment for meeting your needs and the relationship in general. As your relationship grows, show him you're not trying to monopolize his entire world. You should show a sincere interest in what's important to him by encouraging him to participate in those things he loves.

Some things men care about can seem completely silly to you, but if you see that glow in his eyes when he experiences whatever it may be, you've got to register that in your head and see to it he doesn't miss out. There are a number of men who want to be married or in a strong, committed relationship, but many of them are terrified of losing these little nuggets of joy and freedom. What you don't want to do is allow your relationship to interfere with the things for which he has a true passion. You may observe his love for playing golf or spending the weekend fishing or taking time alone to quietly read a book. Would it really kill you to allow your man to spend innocent time doing what he loves? It always amazes me how a woman can have no man for years and when she gets one, she acts like she can't breathe without him. Let him breathe. Whatever his passions may be, find them, then show your support for them and make it easy for him to experience them. Trust me, he will love you for it. This way he feels that he has the best of both worlds—dependence on your love and a degree of independence. He has you *and* he has the things he thought he would have to give up. Women like to talk about how men want to have their cake and eat it too, right? Well, give him a little *peace* of that.

A Brother and His Mother

Most men have a very special relationship with their mother; this is especially true if they grew up without a father at home. With no man in the house, young boys are usually brought up one of two ways. First, he could come from a situation where his mother felt sorry for him because his father wasn't around. This means she catered to his every need and, as many people might interpret it, spoiled him. When the boy matures, in much the same way that his mother provided for him while he was younger, he grows up with an unfailing devotion to providing for her. In the second scenario, mothers raise their sons to be fiercely independent, forcing them to assume the responsibilities typically reserved for the man of the house, but at a much younger age than they should. They are expected to provide for and protect the family. Since there is no father to raise her son to be a man, the mother takes extreme measures to see to it that he is a better man than his father was. In either case, these men develop a powerful bond with their mother. This is the reality for a large number of men in this country, and women must understand this.

Bring peace to his life by making a "sheroic" attempt to get along with his mother. That's usually a lot easier said than done, I know. Some mothers-in-law can be as mean as a junkyard dog when it comes to their sons. You could be an angel from heaven, wings and all, and still not be good enough for some mothers' sons. Try to keep in mind it's nothing personal against you; it's just all about him. She wants to see him happy, and she wants someone to care for him as she would. As quiet as it's kept, most men want their wives to care for them like their mother did.

Don't buck the system. Don't attempt to dismantle everything she's spent a lifetime putting together. Why reinvent the wheel? That means to tailor the way you do some things to how his mother may do them. If she cooks him scrambled eggs and bacon for breakfast, don't try to make him eat a bagel and lox. If he's accustomed to eating on china, don't try being economical and feed him on paper plates. His mother has spent a lifetime with your man and knows many things about him you may not. It's said, "Pride is the mask of one's own faults." Don't let pride lead you down the wrong path. Too many women make that mistake of trying to do their own thing instead of consulting their man's mother. Even if you already know the answer, patronize her by asking. It makes her feel like she has a special place in your life too.

Every woman needs to make sure she understands this dynamic with men. If you fail to take it into consideration, you could be on your way out before you're ever in. Your man knows his mother may be bordering on impossible; however, he will notice and appreciate your efforts, and value you even more for bringing a little more peace to his life.

The Power of the Pamper

Throughout this book I have tried to stress the importance of keeping the piece. I feel it is the most important thing a single woman should do in order to gain the love and respect she is due from a man. I have also presented a number of options that add spice and excitement to a relationship without actually giving him a piece. It is very important for a piece keeper to define her limits. But at the same time she needs to let her man feel that she's taking care of him too. A man will not be content and will constantly explore those limits unless you become an expert in making him feel loved and special while asking him to uphold the piece. Pampering him both physically and mentally will be your number one tool to help you keep his mind off the booty.

I like to equate pampering to pride of ownership. I've found it's easier for women to comprehend this issue if I put it in objective terms to which they can relate. Imagine working fifty hours a week for two years, planning, saving, and dreaming of the day you will be able to buy that shiny new car you've always wanted. For years you never thought you'd be able to afford it, so you'd go to the dealership and look at it through the window and read about it in magazines. Now you're ready to buy. When you pick it up from the dealership you are ultracareful not to wreck it. When you pick up your girlfriends you make sure they wipe their feet so as not to get the carpet dirty. While making a run to the grocery store, instead of parking in the open spot right in front with a car on both sides, you decide to park it at the back of the lot in order to keep other cars from hitting it. As you get out of your new ride, you close the door by giving it a little bump of the hip so you don't get fingerprints on it. Finally, you meticulously change the oil and get it washed weekly. That's what is called pride of ownership.

Since you worked so hard to get it, you take extra care in maintaining it.

I think you can see where I'm going with this. That same care and meticulousness should apply to the special man you're dating. You've dreamed about the kind of man you want. You've worked hard to stick to your values and keep the piece. Now that you've found him, what are you going to do to keep him? How you pamper a man when you're dating and how you pamper him when you're married are very similar, but I will touch more on marriage pampering in Chapter 7. While you're still in the dating phase, the secret is to rely on your nurturing spirit. The following is a list of pampering secrets that will keep your man's engine running and build loyalty in his heart. These are not first date techniques. These are used after you have established an exclusive relationship.

1. Pet him. Remember what I said about the puppy? When you're riding in the car or watching a movie, take your hand and rub his head. Gently play with his ears. Rub his back. Rub his stomach. Do not rub in a way that will make him think he's about to get some.

2. I know it sounds a bit old-school, but grab a comb and scratch his scalp.

3. If he's had a hard day at work, find some baby oil and rub his feet.

4. Run his bath water. Turn on some soothing music. Set his favorite beverage or book by the tub. Again, don't get caught up. You have no business in there while he's taking a bath. But there's nothing wrong with preparing it for him.

5. Show you care about his appearance. Be careful not to be critical or nag. Suggest an outfit for him to wear and make a comment like, "You look fabulous when you wear your black suit and red tie." Another nurturing secret that goes a long way is to do an inspection before he's about to walk out the door. Even if he looks impeccable, straighten his tie, dust off his coat, get his favorite moisturizer and put it on his face. Didn't I tell you men like a little mothering?

6. Make him a lunch and bring it to his job. If he travels, call the hotel and have them deliver breakfast to his room.

7. Go out to dinner and feed him his dessert.

8. Leave a handwritten note under his pillow wishing him sweet dreams and telling him you'll see him the next day.

9. Clip and file his nails from time to time.

10. Prepare his favorite meal for him.

These are just a few ideas, but there are many things you can do to pamper your man and make him feel special. When it comes to pampering, spending a lot of money is unnecessary.

If you look back at the ten things I just listed, they may cost you a total of less than fifty dollars. It's the little things that go an incredibly long way in getting him to preserve a place for you in his heart.

CHAPTER SIX

The New School Woman

YOU SEE HER EVERY DAY. SHE'S NORMALLY SINGLE, BUT EVERY now and then you might get a glimpse of one who's married before she experiences the inevitable divorce. She's usually a well-educated, well-dressed, well-traveled career woman. She's assertive, confident, and can probably "leap tall buildings in a single bound." By many people's standards she's the poster child of success. However, this woman is frustrated with relationships, and relationships are frustrated with her. Everyone and everything is to blame for why she can't get or keep a man. She likes to be in charge and call the shots. She's looking for a fifty-fifty relationship. She thrives on competition and welcomes the next challenge. Status and position are of great importance. The acquisition of material goods and wealth are her priority. Children are merely trophy pieces, similar to many of her other accomplishments that were attained, then placed on a shelf for safekeeping. Her career just doesn't afford her the time to adequately deal with a husband or a child. She ultimately wants a husband, but there just aren't enough good men left on earth who measure up to her standards. This woman represents all the shortcomings of the women's liberation movement. If you're too young to know about that, it was the movement that forced women to the forefront of the workforce.

Don't get me wrong, the women's liberation movement brought about a number of great changes in America. It allowed women the opportunity to achieve never before seen positions of wealth, leadership, and status. It gave young girls the confidence to believe they could achieve anything their hearts desired. It helped close the wage gap and earned women equal pay for equal work. It also produced a stronger, more diverse workforce. It truly changed our country and our world.

However, all of the changes weren't necessarily for the better. It strengthened the workforce, but it has devastated the family. Many women have subconsciously and consciously placed career, status, and money above the family on their list of priorities. That's not necessarily a bad thing, if your goal in life is to remain single and forego having children. The New School woman attempts to do it all—the true jack-of-all-trades. She's the consummate multitasker. But when you attempt to do everything, you often do nothing well, which is evident by America's ever-increasing divorce rate and the staggering decline in the number of marriages. More people are choosing to remain single. The reasons can vary greatly, but I believe the primary one is because expectations have changed so dramatically that it has put undue strain on the relationships between men and women. The gender lines are so blurred no one knows who's driving this wayward ship.

I see mothers investing large amounts of time and effort into their careers at the expense of their families. The interesting part is that those same mothers appear to be baffled as to why their husband cheats or their children stray off the desired path. I see mothers who choose to work overtime to buy a new pair of shoes instead of choosing to invest more time in their children's education. I see women who compete with their husbands rather than arming them with the support and encouragement to compete outside the home. I see women who give their best to "the man," and give what little is left over to *their* man. Ultimately, what I see is a need for change and a reassessment of what's truly important.

Relationships aren't the only areas showing cracks from overextended women. Babies are suffering from a lack of vested supervision, care, and nurturing. No one should have a greater interest in a child's upbringing than the parents. However, in this day and age babies are being raised by nannies, day care workers, and babysitters who stand in for mothers who are out pursuing the American Dream. The caregivers often have more influence over children during their critical stages of development than their parents do. In order for mothers to justify the countless hours their children spend being raised by others, they say they are sending the baby to "school" or "to play with the other children." If there were more mothers at home raising their children, there would be a whole neighborhood of children to play with. Children would also be able to learn much more from spending time with a parent. Mothers desperately research day cares, looking for the most affordable tuition while at the same time searching for the lowest child-to-caregiver ratio. What's a better ratio than one-on-one time with their mothers? Aren't children supposed to be our most cherished treasures? If so, why are they entrusted to what often amounts to minimum-wage workers? Your child learns the day care's values, their routines, their rules, and you're the one forced to conform to what is being taught by the caregiver because you spend the least amount of time with the child. To the caregiver, looking after your child is merely a job. If that's not enough, consider the cost of child care and compare it to the income many mothers receive in return. Is it really worth it? I don't think so. Who ultimately loses? The child.

School-age children aren't doing much better. Often they are required to come home from school to a parentless home. They have to let themselves in, find something to eat, do their homework, and complete chores until their parents make it home from work. In many cases, the parents might not come home for hours after their children arrive. Other children have to stay in after-school care until their parents make it to pick them up. Teachers are being forced to take up the slack where parents are falling short. They teach morals and values and about hygiene, they counsel on dating and sex, and they motivate and discipline. It's difficult to say you're adequately upholding your responsibilities as a parent when the children are basically being raised by others or even raising themselves. They sleep at least eight hours a day, they dedicate at least eight hours to school, and they're at home for three hours or more before a parent even gets home from work. At best, the New School woman spends five out of twenty-four hours with her child. By the time she arrives home from work, she's tired and needs time to unwind, which leaves even less quality time for the child. America is always looking for reasons why the jails are overflowing, teens have no respect for authority, and babies are giving birth to babies, but the answer is right under our noses. It may take a village to raise a child, but how is it possible when the village is busy making money?

It's Raining Men . . . Not

The New School woman can't seem to get much love from men, either. Many of these women don't have to concern themselves with children yet because it's hard enough to find a man. Men are more than willing to indulge in a piece or two, but finding one willing to commit to a relationship is hard to come by and even harder to maintain. That is partly due to the fact that most men aren't interested in the fifty-fifty relationship for which she's looking. Even then, she can't seem to fathom why men aren't falling at her feet. After all, she has a good job, her own house, a car, and a master's degree. Maybe there really aren't enough good men to go around, or maybe they're just not interested in what she has to offer. Whatever the reasons may be, her lack of success with men is primarily self-inflicted. The sooner she figures out why the other three fingers are pointing at her while she's pointing the finger of blame at men, the sooner she can move on to the things that really matter in life. Here are a few things to consider:

A PLAYMATE, BUT NOT A SOUL MATE

The New School woman is a prime candidate to be taken advantage of. Why? First of all, many of them have no man, but desperately want one. They have men who come around from time to time, if you know what I mean. An opportunistic man can sniff out desperation like a bloodhound. Desperation leads to a willingness to do whatever it takes to get a man's attention. As we talked about in Chapter 4, giving up a piece is usually the first thing a woman does when she wants to get a man's attention, especially when she's desperate. But I can almost guarantee that she won't keep him. You can never get the man you want when you show desperation. If you don't have what it takes to be his woman, he's going to take what he can get.

Second, the New School woman is ideal for those men who have wives or girlfriends and are looking for someone with whom to cheat. Think about it. She's already showing desperation, and that means she's probably willing to accept being second in a man's life. Some women actually feel that a part of a man is better than no man at all. That's just the mentality we've got to get rid of if women ever intend to move to their rightful position of power. Nevertheless, married men see this type of woman as an easy target. Her car, her house, and her degrees are signs to him that she has a vested interest in keeping things on the hush-hush. If a man is going to cheat, he's going to try to do it with someone who's not going to show up on his family's doorstep the next morning. Consider yourself warned. Keeping the piece really shouldn't sound like that bad of an option right about now.

Don't play yourself. Do the right thing, and save yourself the headaches and the heartaches—better alone than poorly accompanied. If you're going to work to afford yourself the finer things in life, put forth the work to attain a man who reflects your standards. Coworkers, girlfriends, and platonic guy friends are a nice complement for the career woman, but none of them can replace the joy of a fruitful relationship.

TIME IS OF THE ESSENCE

Time is one of the most important elements required by a man. If a woman doesn't have it to invest in her relationship, the bond will eventually crumble. If she doesn't make space in her schedule for quality interaction with her children, they will falter too. There is simply no substitute for spending quality time with your family. And it's the one thing the New School woman can't spare much of. Everyone in her life has their allotted hour. But being able to buy your child the latest computer game will never replace trips with you to the park. Working long hours to afford to buy your man the hottest new sports car on the market will not stop him from seeing another woman. Time only allows you one opportunity; it will march on, with or without you. And when you're old and gray, the love of your spouse and children can never be second to any of the material goods you've acquired over a lifetime. As women take on more demanding roles in the workplace, time is what they're sacrificing most. That's why they experience so much difficulty in getting and keeping a man.

A real man needs your time, not your money. Take, for instance, a well-established man; we'll call him Tony. He owns a home, a couple of cars, has good investments, is smart, good-looking, spiritual, and trustworthy. That should cover most of the primary things women look for in a man. Now here you come, beautiful, fit, master's degree, homeowner, upwardly mobile career woman climbing the corporate ladder. You work ten hours a day, commute an hour each way, regularly bring work home, and are sometimes required to go on short business trips out of the city. By most people's standards, you've got it going on. But here's your competition; we'll call her Kim. She's equally beautiful, fit, a college graduate, works as an interior designer, and lives in an apartment. She's self-sufficient, sets her own hours, and lives a relatively simple life. How would Tony go about making his decision as to who would ultimately be his woman?

Like most men, Tony is initially captivated by your beauty, so he approaches you and asks you out on a date. It takes you about ten minutes to go through your calendar trying to figure out when your schedule will allow you to get away for lunch or dinner. That's the first sign of trouble. Later in the week he tries to call, but he regularly gets your voice mail. When he does get through, you're distracted because you have work to get done, and you need to get a good night's sleep before your alarm wakes you up at six A.M. to start your workday. Troubling sign number two. Keep in mind, you only have about four hours left in your day after work and sleep, if you're lucky. In that time, you've got to pay bills, work out, run errands, and do whatever work you might have brought home that you need to finish by the next day. If you're really lucky, you might have time to fit in a brief phone call or two. Nevertheless, he manages to get you out for dinner, which was no small feat. Unfortunately, he shows up five minutes late, and instead of you being minimally flexible, you're completely bent out of shape and frustrated with his lack of promptness. The troubling trends continue. In conversation he learns you do not cook, you have a housekeeper, you want children someday, and you're going out of town on a business trip next weekend. I think you get the picture.

Now what do you think Tony's overall impression of you is? I'd say not very good. He may keep you as a friend for networking or a midnight booty call, but definitely not a wife. Most women value having a family more than a career, but I find it quite strange why they invest more time, energy, preparation, and education in their careers than they do in a family. Most successful women want successful men, but they've invested so much time and energy in their careers, they have very little of what a successful man needs—time—and an abundance of what he doesn't—money. If you really want a successful man, you need to bring something to the table he doesn't already have. Men want women who know their way around the house. Men want women who can be good mothers and make them feel like kings. They want their wives to provide a home environment that's a resting place—their own little hideout. It should protect husbands from the stresses of the world.

So again I ask, what do you really feel you can offer him? He realizes he will be competing with your job for time. He can deduce you're probably not very useful around the house. You've got just about all of the material things anyone could ever want, which leaves very little room for him to spoil you. You want children, but he's wondering who's going to take care of them. The outlook is bleak at best.

Tony later approaches Kim. They agree to meet for lunch. Kim works about six hours a day, but can take a day off at her discretion. She works from her home office and very seldom travels out of town for business. When Tony gets off work, Kim's day has already started to wind down. In conversation, Tony learns that Kim loves to have dinner parties at her apartment, has never traveled outside of the country, and wants to one day have two children and continue to work from home doing what she loves. She likes to watch football on Sundays, and actually volunteered to help him prepare a presentation for work.

The future with Kim is in full, high-definition, vivid color. Why? Because she has things she can offer him, the biggest being time. Tony doesn't need more money or material things—of course those are always nice, but they're not needed. He's looking for a companion. Kim also makes

Tony feel needed, which is a very important characteristic, and one to which men are attracted. Tony likes the fact that she works and is doing something she loves. It makes him feel comfortable to know she's not just waiting on a meal ticket. Kim can actually make Tony's life better because she takes pride in providing a stable home and raising children. If you can't make a man's life better, and he can't make yours better, why bother? You can do bad all by yourself.

To sum this all up, don't let your career use you up. There is so much more to life. If you want a meaningful relationship, you must be able to fill a need in a man's life. It's very hard to do this if you're consumed with your own needs. Time is critically important, and it's usually the one thing the New School woman can't afford to sacrifice. Analyze what it is you're bringing to the relationship. If the only thing is a piece, your days in that relationship are numbered. That's something that can be found on any street corner.

In order for the New School woman to get a real man, she needs to consider a career with more flexible work hours. Working is a good thing, but consider career fields that are less demanding of your time or that can be accomplished from your home office. This will help to more effectively manage the time challenges presented when attempting to balance family and career. The growth of computers and the

Internet has all but eliminated the need to go to a job and work five days a week. Many jobs can now be done from the convenience of home. Whether you want to work or have to work, if you value having a family or a relationship, strive to find a way to spend most of your workday at home, even if it's in your home office. You owe it to your family.

INTIMIDATED OR JUST REPULSED?

"*The reason I'm single is because men are intimidated by me. I have my own stuff. The jewelry I wear, I bought it. The house I live in and the car I drive, I bought them too. I don't need a man.*"

As long as you have that kind of attitude you'll never have a man. No! Nothin'! Nada! You may intimidate a small percentage of men with your fame, authority, or beauty. An even smaller percentage of men may be threatened by the fact that you have your own "stuff." I'll reluctantly give you that one. However, the majority of eligible men aren't fazed by a common, gainfully employed woman. A boy may be minimally impressed, but a man, I don't think so. This excuse is a cop-out these women use to justify their undesirability. I, personally, have never met a man who was intimidated by a woman because of her "independence." *Repulsed* is the more accurate word that comes to my mind.

A man will not allow a woman to disparage him, but often, that's exactly what the New School woman does. She radiates "I don't need you" without ever opening her mouth. A man is not going to stand for that type of attitude from anyone. Who would, for that matter? Imagine if you worked for a company to which you gave your very best year after year, but the owner constantly made you feel like you weren't needed. How are you going to react? You're probably going to either quit or stop giving your all. That's basically what men have resigned themselves to doing with these types of women. Confidence is great, but arrogance is a nuisance.

Just because you attain a degree of success doesn't give you the right to look down your nose at anyone. Try offering a hand up instead of stepping over a person you feel isn't where they should be. That's one of the reasons why men can't appreciate your accomplishments. It's not that they're looking at your car, your house, and your degrees and saying, "Whoa, she's too good for me." They're more likely to judge you based on your attitude and how you interpret your own success.

These women also tend to be the instigators of competition in a household. They want to bring attention to their significance based on the percentage of income they bring to the home. They try to evaluate whose career carries the most importance when it comes to divvying up household duties. The New School woman wants her status taken into consideration by her man. She likes to measure her accomplishments against his.

A man's woman, his wife, his girlfriend, or his mate should be a source of encouragement, inspiration, and vitalization. The home should be a haven safe from competition and the rigors of the world. The last thing men want to do is scrape and fight every day to earn the respect of their peers, only to have to come home and compete with their wife. I don't think so. He'd rather slide down a razor blade into a puddle of alcohol.

Stop accusing men of being intimidated by you, and accept the fact that you may not be what they're looking for. As long as the blame is being placed on the man, you minimize your own contribution to the outcome. If you're not getting the type of attention you feel you deserve from men, start by analyzing the positive attributes you bring to a man's life. Don't forget, material things are merely the gravy.

The Fifty-Fifty Relationship

It doesn't exist. The New School woman sees herself as an equal to her man and feels everything should be split fifty-fifty. Since she has a career also, she sees no reason why her man can't split the household duties. Raising children is no different. If the baby needs attention, her man better be prepared for his turn. I hate to burst your bubble, but the last time I checked, men and women weren't built the same. Their skill sets, as the corporate people like to say, just aren't the same. As we discussed in Chapter 2, everything about a woman is different from a man, so why would you feel it necessary for a man to serve the same function you do? That's part of the reason why you're manless; you're looking for that pot of gold at the end of the rainbow. It just doesn't exist.

Notice, I never said women were less than men. I merely said they were not equals. This argument seems to get misinterpreted every time it's brought up. My message shouldn't be taken as demeaning or degrading. It's simply stating the obvious. You don't use a hammer for a screwdriver's job. That's why it's important for you and your man to embrace your roles in a relationship. It allows things to run more smoothly. For example, if a man knows he's responsible for the upkeep and maintenance of the cars and the exterior of the house, there's nothing wrong with him expecting his wife to take care of the inside. That's not saying duties won't overlap from time to time, but it's more efficient if each person understands his or her own responsibilities and how they contribute to the whole. When you're working for a corporation, the CEO doesn't lay out all the duties required to run the company and tell his employees to divide them up equally and make sure everything gets done. There's an accountant, a janitor, a lawyer, and an engineer, and everyone is required to perform the duties they're best equipped to do. Why should the family be any different?

I DON'T NEED A MAN

One of the greatest tragedies that has come about since the rise of the New School woman is her desire to have children out of wedlock. When these women reach a state of complete despair by realizing they may never find a suitable man, which in turn means they will not experience the joy of having children with a husband, some are choosing to get pregnant without the consent of their male partners. This is the ultimate form of selfishness. It not only puts the unsuspecting man in a difficult position, but it deprives the child of the opportunity to grow up in a traditional family. If they're willing to stoop to these depths, wouldn't it be more logical to make finding the right husband a greater priority than climbing the corporate ladder? Some do, however, choose to adopt. And that is a viable option. The world would be much better served by you adopting one of the thousands of children in need of loving parents, than having some man that you barely even like permanently imbedded to your life because you made the independent decision to get pregnant.

How Did We Get Here?

My theory is that the New School woman has bought into the so-called American Dream. The pursuit of wealth and materialism has fogged her vision and she has lost her way. Managing a successful family just isn't as chic as it used to be, and society has convinced many women that solely being a wife and a mother is underachieving. Women continue to strive and attain incredible positions of status, power, and wealth at the expense of their families. In order to attain and maintain these types of powerful positions, the New School woman has developed professional characteristics that are critical to her survival in the business world. For example, she must be very pragmatic, shrewd, assertive bordering on aggressive, and analytical. She may even downplay her femininity in an effort to portray a more professional exterior. These are often the same traits that turn men off because they're very masculine in nature. Men are most often attracted to women who are more delicate and feminine. Men like to be in charge and look for women who know how to feed into their masculinity.

The problem is the New School woman is not very adept at leaving those traits at work. She wants to bring her status and power home with her, which inevitably causes problems. You may be Judge, Captain, or Dr. Smith at work, but when you get home, you are Mrs. Smith to your man. Your position at work should not come into play when dealing with issues in your relationship. The New School woman actually feels as though she is entitled to call the shots in her relationship because of the money she makes and the position she holds at work. Think about it this way: If you were to set your career aside and your man were to do the same, he's still a man and you're still a woman, and you must work together using the complementary gifts God gave you.

The second half of my theory is this: Due to the fact that women value financial security, status, and power in a man, they incorrectly assume men value those same characteristics in women. That couldn't be further from the truth. The very nature of a man is to be a protector and provider, so why would he need you to protect and to provide? That's like a bird needing an airplane. Why would it fly in an airplane if it can fly itself? Most accomplished men are living where they want to live, driving what they want to drive, and doing the things that they enjoy doing. So, why would he need your six-figure income? This is why so many successful women attract needy men, because they need what you're offering. I can't tell you the number of times a woman has approached me and asked to be set up with one of the men I know, and the first attribute she touts is her job and her education. So? Now what? A man looks for a woman who has complementary traits. He needs her to be what he's not. She should be nurturing, gentle-spirited, soft-spoken, smart, sexy, and attractive, to name a few. I did say *sexy* and *attractive*. Never forget that men are visual creatures and need to have someone to be with who's a pleasure to the eyes. To a man, a pretty box makes the contents even more appealing. That's assuming there are contents. Think about the number of successful men who marry women who don't have money. That proves a woman's money is not at the top of a man's list of priorities. A man likes a woman who knows how to make him feel like a man, not one who challenges his manhood. It's not that having a successful woman wouldn't be nice, but that's more like the gravy, not the meat and potatoes.

"*I don't know what you're talkin' about. Just about every man I meet is more interested in what I do for a living and wants to know how much money I make.*" The problem is you're dealing with the wrong type of boy. A real man won't feel comfortable with you working to support him. He may be interested in knowing you have some sort of work ethic, goals, direction, and drive, but he shouldn't be expecting you to take care of him. A real man's goal is for his wife not to have to work. If she wants to work, that's a different thing altogether. But don't allow yourself to be pimped! If you're leaving the house to go to your job every day, he better be going to one as well. If he doesn't have a job, he better be looking for one for the same number of hours you commit to doing yours. It's a good thing women have the power to accept or deny a man's advances because if you're stuck with a man you're taking care of who doesn't want to work, at least you can feel comfort in knowing that you chose him.

No Love Lost

Now that I've had the opportunity to discuss some of the reasons why the New School woman isn't as desirable as she might think, it's important to discuss where to go from here. This is not a simple issue to fix because it touches on just about every stage of development in a woman's life. It can be your upbringing, high school and college years, or professional life—each stage of development will require some out-of-the-box thinking to bring more balance to the New School woman's life. The next few pages will outline a plan, not only for the current generation, but also for the generations to come.

It starts with mothers changing the mind-sets and priorities with which they raise children. Then as their children reach what I call the planning years, parents need to present them with numerous options and guide them as they start to make their own decisions. When these children reach the implementation years, they have a much better opportunity to live the life that's right for them, instead of what someone else thought was the best thing. Money and materialism can't be the primary focus because money can't make you happy.

The first steps in making this change is to acknowledge that the New School woman is not just an individual problem—it's one that affects the whole society. How a child is raised can either benefit or take away from our communities, so it's important for the community to have an interest in the children they produce. A child needs to learn to respect authority, and that starts with respecting parents first. With that being said, each family has the ability to positively or negatively affect our way of life, simply through the time they invest in their children. It's not good enough to merely be present with children. Children need to be taught, molded, and groomed. Money is important, but it can't be the only thing families have passion about. No one—and I mean absolutely no one—should have a more vested interest in your children than you. A strong family is the foundation of a strong country.

UPBRINGING

Early Years

Many women have been mistreated or have seen someone they're close to suffer due to the actions of a man. Mistreatment comes in many different forms—physical abuse, emotional abuse, cheating, divorce, etc. However, when those women have daughters, they often teach them about men based on their own experiences. If her man cheated, she teaches her daughters not to trust men. If he left her with no financial means to take care of herself, she teaches her daughters to be independent.

Most young children think their parents are the smartest people in the world. They take their word as gospel because they know nothing else. Some mothers' teachings are emotionally based, which can limit a child's development if not put in the proper context. There's nothing wrong with telling the truth, but avoid making broad generalizations. You should never teach your children that all men cheat just because their daddy was a cheater, for example. They don't understand the concept of generalization. They can't come to the conclusion that mommy's heart was broken, and she really didn't mean what she said. Nevertheless, the children grow up with these types of negative perceptions of men or negative perceptions of relationships in general, and it's very difficult for men to break the shackles those preconceived notions can put on a relationship.

Instead, parents ought to take a more objective approach, teaching the costs and the benefits of certain decisions. In the case of the New School woman, many of them have been taught to go to college so they can get a good job. This is the root of the problem because parents rarely explain the sacrifices required by that decision. College is a must, but it has to have more meaning than working for someone for the rest of your life. Children go throughout their entire lives really feeling like they're doing the right thing, but instead of living out their own dreams, they live the dreams of their parents by going to school to get a good job. I think it's important to know your options and explore them before making a commitment to a particular path in life. Just because your mother felt it was a good thing to do doesn't mean it's right for you.

The same goes for teaching young girls not to depend on men. All men aren't cheaters, and most men wouldn't leave their wife and children with nothing. We must depend on each other. If you can't trust a man to take care of his family, that's probably not the man you should be with. Don't forget, ultimately you're the one who chooses him. If a man can't trust you to be a good mother and wife, you're probably not the one for him, either. I'm just saying that it's important for children to be given options and to be taught the consequences and benefits of their decisions.

I think more parents should teach their children to pursue happiness. When your purpose in life is to find out what makes you happy, then your whole outlook changes. The only way to know what makes you happy is to understand the consequences and benefits of your options. Know what it is you want and go after it. Your son can't know that going to college and getting a good job is right for him unless he first understands that one of its biggest cons is that his employer will basically dictate when, where, and how he lives his life. Being a business owner may be more fitting and fulfilling for him. Don't limit your child's destiny, but teach him there are positives and negatives associated with everything. Allow him to choose his direction. As the saying goes, "Choose a job you love, and you will never have to work a day in your life." In order to attain that state of happiness, you first have to lay out a path to follow.

PLANNING YEARS

Teens to twenty-five years old

This is crunch time. By the time you become a teenager you need to start sorting through your thoughts in order to set a plan in motion for your life. Analyze what sincerely makes you happy. Though money is important, it's not quite as important when you're doing something you love. College is not optional. Look at it as the bare minimum level of education required for life itself. You may feel you will never use a lot of the things you're being taught, and you may not, but that's beside the point. Education makes you a better person and a more productive citizen. In this day and age, it's crucial. High school just isn't enough. A college degree allows you more options in life. No matter what path you decide to take—a family or a job—you should be sufficiently educated.

If you already know what really makes you happy, develop a plan to make it happen and put that plan into motion. When you're young it doesn't matter if you start out in one direction and change your mind later. Everyone changes as they grow older, and no matter how old you are, you will come to find that everyone has an opinion about how you should live your life, and that's fine. It's important that you always take the time to listen and learn. It costs you absolutely nothing to listen to what others have to say. It may truly be valuable information, but you can't know unless you listen. The young people who are good listeners are the ones who usually excel in life. If you're one of those people who have to learn through experience only, life can be very tough. Learn from others' experiences when you can. Take in as much information from as many different sources as possible before you begin to outline the steps of your future. It will open your eyes to the world.

Regardless of what path you decide to take, it's important to sort out where starting a family fits into your list of priorities. It is the one decision you can't take back. Once you have children, you can't put them on layaway to pick up at a later date. If you don't invest time with them, you can't ask for a do-over in order to be a better parent the second time around. If you give everything to your career and never give a good man a chance, you may never have the opportunity to have children when you're older. This is one of the most important decisions you'll ever make. You can always go back to school and get another degree, and you can always start another business or get a different job, but when you choose to start a family, the benefits extend well past your lifetime.

Before you can make that type of decision, there are a few things you need to think about. One school of thought

I want you to be aware of is the "work first and grow your family later" approach. I'll call that option 1. This is when you stay in school to acquire more advanced degrees, such as a master's or doctoral degree, then enter the workforce to attain a certain level of success before you dedicate time to a husband or children.

The other school of thought is the "grow your family first and work later" approach. I'll call that option 2. This is when you get married and have children before thirty years of age or so, and enter the workforce after your children are established in school. Both approaches have their pros and cons, and it's up to you to figure out which one is most appropriate for you.

Here are just a few of the costs and benefits of each option.

Option 1—work first and grow your family later

1. You can obtain your education and training at a younger age, broadening your opportunities.
2. You can possibly retire sooner with more money.
3. You can enjoy the fruits of your labor while you're young, able, and strong. You can enjoy many things your body might not allow once you're older.

(continued)

4. You can have more earning years.
5. Your options in men are fewer. A large percentage of them are married, divorced, or have children.
6. Men are forced to deal with your infamous ticking clock, which shows your level of desperation.
7. The probability of birth complications go up dramatically as you age.
8. Your body may not be as capable of having children the older you get.
9. You're not as youthful and may not be able to participate in as many of your child's activities as you once could have.
10. Many professionals are immediately forced back to work six weeks after giving birth, leaving their baby to depend on a caregiver.

Option 2—grow your family first and work later

1. Your body is better equipped for a faster recovery from multiple pregnancies.
2. Due to your youthfulness, you will be prepared to keep up with a child's high state of energy.
3. You're young enough to reestablish a substantial career after your children have gone to school.
4. You have a much larger pool of eligible men your age from which to choose.
5. There is a better chance of finding someone who loves you for you and not your wealth—or lack thereof.

6. You and your husband can grow your material wealth together.
7. You enter the workforce late and may require additional schooling and training.
8. You may be a less reliable employee because you have children who come before the job.
9. You may not be mature enough to choose a good husband. Inexperience often leads to poor decision making.
10. Your financial security may be lacking at a time when there's a great demand for it.

As you can see, there are a number of things to consider when deciding which path best suits you, but it's important that you start thinking about it sooner rather than later. You may be one of the few people who have no desire to marry at all. In that case your planning is considerably simpler: You do what makes you happy. There are times in life when you may feel that staying single or not having children is what you want, but those feelings may be associated with some type of unpleasant experience. Very few people are designed to remain happily single, so if you feel that a family may not be right for you, take a little time to explore the experiences that may have led you to that type of thinking.

Many young ladies make decisions without ever knowing why they chose the path they did or what consequences are associated with it. They have children early in life, then feel they've missed out on their youth, or they dedicate their life to their career then find out they feel empty without a family. I believe that's why the New School woman's life isn't ultimately fulfilling. She took a path early in life without giving full thought to the result. She then got to a point where she simply had to salvage what she had. Weigh your options, make a plan, and put the plan into motion.

IMPLEMENTATION YEARS

Twenty-five and older

Once you feel comfortable with your plan, then you've got to implement it. Whether you're twenty-nine or "many-nine" years old, you should have a distinct plan you're in the process of implementing. Many women often lose focus of the overall goal and settle for any old piece of man instead of the man they ultimately desire. They also get frustrated when they're not getting immediate results. The key is to not get overwhelmed with the big picture. It's okay to envision yourself with the loving husband of your dreams, two or three children, and the house with the picket fence, but it will appear much easier to get there if you focus on one step at a time. To paraphrase Martin Luther King, Jr., "You do not need to see the entire staircase. All you need to see is the next step."

Step one: Educate yourself about men. The fact that you're reading this book is a great start and puts you far ahead of most women who have to bump their heads before learning that the floor is hard. But don't stop there. Learn all you can about the things that really make relationships work, like intimacy and the dynamics of communication. Beware of women trying to teach you about men; learn about men from men. Guy friends are a great resource. Some women study for years to excel in a particular career field. Shouldn't you display the same, if not more, determination in preparing yourself for your family?

Step two: Focus on marrying the right man sooner rather than later. The first five years after college are a great time to start narrowing your search. I call that period the glory years. That's because there is an abundance of men who are single, available, and have no children. This is also the time most young people are still relatively broke and in the process of establishing themselves financially. That's important to know because money changes people. It also makes it easier to establish whether a person loves you for you or loves you for what you have. It's terrible to have to put it that way, but it is what it is. These days many people have a what-can-you-do-for-me attitude.

The last thing you want to do is put yourself in the predicament of being the New School woman. Knowing that family is your priority, you don't want to eliminate most of the male population when you decide to put a husband on your wish list. Imagine the choices with which you would be left if you dedicated your glory years to your career and delayed finding the right man until your mid to late thirties. By that time you've probably attained a degree of power, status, and wealth. Then, to make matters worse, you set a personal standard not to date men who aren't in your socio-economic category. Not to forget, most overachieving men aren't looking for overachieving women. That leaves you, well . . . single and desperate.

Step three: Make use of the knowledge you gather in this book to empower your man and grow your family. There's no more important job than raising intelligent, productive, and obedient children. A woman can always assist her man by contributing to the workforce, but a man can never assist his woman with bearing children. Never put anything before your desire to reproduce. The female body brings forth life, and nothing material has any significance without mankind to put it to use.

CHAPTER SEVEN

NO WAR AND "PIECE"

IN THIS CHAPTER WE'RE GOING TO BRING IT ALL TOGETHER BY focusing on the ultimate goal—a happy and fulfilling marriage. A happy marriage brings about an incredible number of benefits in just about every aspect of life: better physical and mental health, financial health, and community health. Children whose parents are happily married tend to be better educated, have fewer behavioral problems, and grow up to be better people. We've spent the last six chapters dissecting relationships and the role women play when they go wrong. We've also discussed a number of secrets women can use to get the most out of the men they care for. Many of the things we've discussed have specifically targeted single women, but married women often face many of the same problems, and in some cases many more if they haven't discovered and taken advantage of their power. In this chapter I'll take the highlights of the previous ones and show you how they relate to marriage. This will ensure your marriage has no war and plenty of "piece."

Dating is important. That's why I've spent so much time talking about it. Don't use it to play house, though. I see people in six-plus-year relationships, and I'm often confused. He either fits or he doesn't. Keep it moving. The only women who stay in relationships that long are the ones who are giving up a piece. Instead, use your experiences as a training ground to gain wisdom before you make a lifetime commitment of marriage. The stronger your dating habits, the more success you'll have in finding Mr. Right. Even then, you'll still come across issues and make some decisions you'll wish you would've handled differently. Keeping the piece will help you to spring back in case you come across the inevitable knucklehead. It's all a part of the growth and maturity required to be a good wife.

You don't want to be one of those women who finds a good man and has no idea what to do to keep him. Never let your guard down. The "cleanup woman" is always willing and ready to step in when you're slackin'. She's the type of woman who waits and watches your marriage unravel when things aren't going as planned, then she steps in where you fell short and steals the man in whom you have invested so much time and effort. That is not what we want to happen, so let's get down to business.

WHAT IS MARRIAGE?

Marriage is a sacred union between a man and a woman specifically designed as a critical part of overall human development. Humans, like most animals, are happier and healthier when they have companions. There are some people who spend a lifetime single, but that's the exception and not the rule. Marriage is also the proper environment for raising children. Don't for a second think that what you're seeing in today's society is normal. There's nothing acceptable about men running around having multiple baby mamas all over the country. There's also nothing acceptable about a woman having multiple kids by different baby daddies. That's why it doesn't work. A child needs a father and a mother. Do not allow yourself to settle for anything else.

If you're ever having a hard time making a decision about life, or about anything for that matter, always do what I call the "mankind test" first. Ask yourself, "Is what I'm about to do going to add something positive to mankind, or is it going to take away from mankind?" In other words, if everyone did what you're about to do, would it cause a major disruption to the population? The first answer that comes to mind will tell you if what you're about to do is right or wrong. Marrying and raising productive, well-rounded children is the right thing to do.

Marriage or Wreckage?

There's a catch to this whole marriage thing: If you want to get married, marry the right person. Sounds simple, right? That's because it is. The concept of marriage is pure; people are the ones who jack up the whole process. They get married to the wrong person at the wrong time for the wrong reasons, then they blame marriage for the train wreck. Don't let the people who have made bad decisions discourage you from one of the greatest joys given to us here on earth. This reminds me of the slogan "Guns don't kill people. People kill people." Well, how about, "Marriage doesn't kill marriage. People kill marriage."

I'll never forget the conversation I had with this group of teenage girls. I just happened to be telling them how wonderful it is to have a family. I was smiling and attempting to encourage them. I told them how fun it is watching children grow up and all the hilarious moments that come along with child development. Then I asked the three girls, kind of expecting a certain answer, "Do you guys want to be married and have children one day?" Their answers changed me forever. One of the girls innocently nodded yes. The second little girl said, "I want to have children, but I don't want to get married." The third girl emphatically said, "I never want to get married. I want to live by myself." I'm sure I looked like I had seen a ghost. I really wanted to leave it alone, but I just had to ask why. In a nutshell, they went on and on about how all the people they know are divorced and all the ones who are married fight all the time.

The heartbreaking part of the whole thing was their outlook on life. I couldn't believe one girl basically already knew she wanted to be a single parent. The other one was almost insulted I asked such a question. But their answers were honest, and I guess I understand because that's the example today's children are given.

So, who is the wrong person to marry? There is no universal answer to that question, but there are a lot of general guidelines to steer you clear of the wreckage.

1. Only marry a man who is also ready to get married. Ready doesn't mean ready to put on suit, ready to buy a ring, or ready to say, "I do." It means ready to make a lifetime commitment, ready to conduct himself with integrity, fidelity, and responsibility, and ready to not only father a child, but to be a father to one.

(continued)

2. Don't marry someone who isn't able to provide for his family. If he doesn't work, doesn't want to work, or even if he's waiting on a settlement, he is not "marry-able." In addition to being a provider, a man must have skills around the house—or at least be motivated to learn. There is nothing worse than a man who has to hire someone to do routine chores—unless of course, he can afford to do so. If he doesn't know how to maintain the family vehicles (change the oil, do minor repairs, fix a flat, wash, and wax), that's grounds to be concerned. If he can't maintain the lawn (cut, plant, fertilize, dig, water), start to pay closer attention. If he has no knowledge of home repairs (painting, minor plumbing, changing a light bulb) . . . next. Can you imagine cooking, cleaning, taking care of kids, and having a man who can't carry his weight? Unacceptable.

3. Don't marry a man who is not the leader. He must be able to prove he's a responsible leader, not by his words, but by his actions.

4. Don't marry a man whose personality, hobbies, and lifestyle are not compatible with yours. People will try to convince you that opposites attract, but I believe that's only temporary. A more accurate cliché is "Birds of a feather flock together." Couples who have more similarities than differences truly have more longevity.

When is the wrong time to marry? There are many. Here are a few to give you a hint the wreckage is right around the corner.

1. Never marry on the rebound. If you or your man is coming out of a breakup, you must give yourself no less than a year to get the other person out of your system. Marriage requires a large degree of maturity, and it's not fair to your new man if your heart and mind are still thinking about your past relationship.
2. Don't get married too young. I can't tell you what age is too young because everyone matures at a different rate. However, I don't think you should even consider marriage until you have graduated from college.
3. Don't marry a man who has not had the time to mature. Remember, men have to get past the playa phase, among other things.
4. Lastly, if you're at a stage in your career that is not going to allow you to fully commit to your family, this is not the time to get married. Realize that working long hours, bringing work home and traveling extensively do not create fertile ground for a healthy relationship. Your marriage and your family have to come before your career.

Getting married for the wrong reasons has to be one of the leading causes of a massive train wreck. Just because you're getting married for all of the right reasons doesn't mean he's doing the same. Here are a few wrong reasons to get married.

1. Never marry a man solely based on how he looks. Beauty fades, and you better have something else that keeps you interested in him.
2. Never marry a man solely based on how he makes you feel physically. There are twenty-four hours in every day, and you should consider yourself lucky if your man can keep you physically stimulated for an hour.
3. Don't marry solely based on his financial capabilities. This is simply a form of prostitution. Don't let a man attempt to buy you. You're worth more than any amount of money he could possibly come up with.
4. Don't marry just because you're pregnant. If you've already made one mistake, why add another one to it? When that child is grown and gone, the last thing you want to do is be stuck with a joker every day whom you don't even love.
5. Don't get married because of parental pressure. They're not the ones who have to interact with him every day. It's your life and you're the one who has to live it.

No Time for Cruise Control

Once you've gotten married, it's party time, a reason for celebration, right? You've made it. You've found Mr. Right, and he's found you. Now you can ride off into the sunset happily ever after . . . I don't think so. That's only partially correct. Celebrating is great, but forever is a long time. The only way you can successfully do anything for the rest of your life is to work at it. Marriage is not something you can necessarily master, but you can constantly get better at it. You should view it as a journey, not a destination. That means you should never consider yourself to have arrived—just enjoy the ride, the bumps, the scenery, the rest stops, the whole thing. The moment you take your husband for granted, you stand the chance of losing everything you have worked for.

Entirely too many women get married and then stop doing the very things that made their man fall in love with them. They think the hard part is over and put on the cruise control. That's a monumental mistake. Need I remind you that there are plenty of single women out there looking for a man just like yours? I know you're probably thinking that there are just as many men out there looking for a wife like you too, right? Wrong. Don't forget, women dream about being married; men dream about having unlimited access to the cat. That means you must constantly work to keep your marriage fresh and exciting. This doesn't necessarily have to be considered a bad thing. It can really be a lot of fun. It's all in how you approach it.

When you're married, you can literally open up a treasure chest of love. This is the time for you to explore and experience a whole new chapter of life. If you were disciplined enough to keep the piece before you got married, you should have plenty of vim and vigor for the journey ahead. This is a level of ecstasy that not too many young ladies ever get the opportunity to experience because these days they don't understand the importance of waiting and sacrificing. These days, a woman making love for the first time on her wedding night is almost as rare as a submarine with screen doors.

Let me see if I can accurately illustrate this for you. Little Johnny sees a beautiful red bicycle he wants on TV. He asks his parents to buy it for him, but they say he must save his money until he is able to buy the bike himself. He's obedient and begins to save his money. Meanwhile, he reads about it, goes to the store to take a closer look, and imagines himself riding it through the neighborhood. After a year—which to a kid seems like forever—of working odd jobs, sacrificing his time, and saving his money, he is able to buy the bicycle. Can you visualize the ecstasy he experienced when he finally got his hands on that bike? He rode like he'd never ridden before, smiling and laughing, waving at all the people as he passed by. Since he had worked so hard to get it, he cleaned it, oiled it, and waxed it weekly because he didn't want it to ever break down. That's what I call "pride of ownership."

Now, how different would this story have been if he decided to take the first bike that came along, which just happened to be the old, rusty one someone had thrown in a Dumpster? It had been ridden so much that whoever owned it before was tired of riding it and had tossed it in the trash. Johnny dusted it off and rode it for a couple of weeks, never really took care of it, and ended up putting it in the corner of the garage because he was bored with it and wanted a new one.

Now, here you are just like Johnny. You see women breaking guys off a piece left and right. Everyone talks about how wonderful it is. Your friends attempt to talk you into trying it. You even imagine yourself doing it from time to time, but you want something special. You could've settled for the first guy who came along, but you decided to sacrifice and wait until you're married. When you finally pledge your life to the man of your dreams, think of the reward you get. You can ride like you've never ridden before, smiling, laughing, and waving at yourself in the mirror. Because you waited, you see to it your husband is not taken for granted, by showing pride of ownership.

Let me go back for just a moment. Follow me as I illustrate the similarities of the bike for which Johnny decided to settle and a piece. Instead of waiting until you were married, you decide to exercise your free will and explore. Let's say Bobby is lucky enough to get a brand-new, beautiful, never-before-ridden piece. Pardon my bluntness, but he rides and rides it until he is tired of riding it, then gets rid of it. Along comes Johnny, who decides it's not really what he wants, but he'll ride it for a little while himself. Well, he doesn't keep it long and sets it aside for a brand-new one. No one wants the old, rusty, used one. They all want the new one.

Before I go any further, let me remind you that it's never too late to get it straight. If you've already given up a piece, that's okay because everything I've just said applies to you too. Don't you dare think you have a special set of nonvirgin rules. If you're single and want to be married, this is the first step in gaining any man's respect. Today is a great day to become a piece keeper. You can't get a different result if you continue doing what you've always done. Need I repeat, better alone than poorly accompanied?

Back to Johnny and the bike. I hope that was enough to get you to understand the importance of waiting. Your husband will be absolutely thrilled to finally get his hands on you, among other things, when you do marry. Then you can really let loose all that was stored up. Here's what I want you to remember. Never play games with the piece. In order to drive this point home, let me repeat, women dream of being married, and men dream of having unlimited access to the cat. After you're married, give him as much as he can handle. You want him to be so saturated with loving he will not want to even consider looking at another woman.

I have never understood why some women choose to ration out the goods to their husbands. If he was a good boy for the week, she'll give him some. If he took out the trash without being asked, she'll give him some. What the heck is that? I know one thing: It's one of the biggest complaints I hear from married and divorced men, by far. They just aren't getting it regularly, and their wives use it like a reward system. Holding the goods hostage is a major no-no. Besides, why on earth would you send your horny husband out into the land of milk and honey to fend for himself? The women who do that kind of thing are the same ones you see on *Jerry Springer* crying big crocodile tears because their man cheated on them. If you don't want him to cheat, give him a reason not to.

A Freak in the Sheets

There's no such thing as a married ho. She's what you call a wife. Well, I guess there are wives who are sleeping with every man but their husband. For argument's sake, let's assume a wife is loyal to her husband. Force yourself to get over whatever hang-ups and inhibitions you might have about sex. As a matter of fact, discuss your fantasies with your husband, and have him share his fantasies with you. Feel free to explore your sexuality. This is the time to stop wondering and start finding out. All those stories you heard when you were in college about freaks doing it in the car, in the park, or in the elevator, and all those loud, quiet, sloppy, wet, sleepy, sneaky, upside-down, right-side-up, leg-over, leg-under, you-name-it sex moves you've dreamed of trying, now is the time for you to go for it.

Speaking of college, I remember a girl all of the guys used to share stories about. She was passed around from guy to guy her whole four years in school. Sometimes I felt like I needed help picking my jaw up off the ground after listening to some of the incredibly wild things she did. I'm telling you, she was all of that and then some. She was a true professional. About ten years after college or so, I happened to talk with her husband—well, ex-husband. When I saw him I assumed he must be happily married, but when I asked about his wife, he informed me that he was divorced. I didn't want to, but I had to ask why. He went on and on about how he couldn't get a piece to save his life. I thought, *That can't possibly be true*. He went on with more of the gory details about how routine and boring things were when they did find their way to the bedroom. I just couldn't believe it. I guess that's what happens when you use up all of your good tricks before you get married.

That brings me to my next point. Giving him as much as he can handle is one thing, but you've got to break away from the daily routine from time to time so you can inject some excitement into your love life. One of the things you might want to consider is accommodating your man's potential desire of having a different piece. Hold on—I'm not saying you should let him go out and do his thing. You don't want an open marriage, but you can accommodate his fantasy of having something different. Of the numerous men I've talked with who cheat, many of them claim they love their wives, but they just wanted something different. Why don't you give him something different before he goes looking for it? This is much more common than you might think. There are many women who claim they did everything right, but their man still cheated. If you didn't consider him needing something different, you didn't do everything right.

"How much difference could there possibly be?" you ask. I say, a lot. To leave no stone unturned, let me explain. Yes, the act of sex may be the same, but there are many things that surround the act that can be different. Wouldn't you hate eating pizza month after month, year after year? I'm not talking about a supreme pizza, stacked with toppings, either. Imagine eating the same ol' cheese pizza. Sex is no different. You've got to add some special ingredients, maybe some chili powder to keep it hot and spicy.

Pay attention because women all over the world have been thirsting for the information I'm about to give you. Have you ever heard guys ranting and raving about how good a woman was in bed and wondered, *Wow, what could she possibly be doing to make these men flip out like this?* It's important for you to understand that your answer can't come from a woman. It's got to come from a man. Some women think they are all that, but guys try to spare their feelings so they don't get cut off the next time. Like I alluded to earlier, how much difference could there really be? The actual act of making love is so basic.

Okay, here's the secret to blowing your husband's mind in bed. Response. It is the single most important thing you can master that will change your love life forever. You've got to give him accurate, immediate, and exciting feedback. Let me explain without getting too graphic. It is essential for a man to perform in order to make love. If he's not aroused and Willy doesn't come to the party, the festivities are over before they ever got started. Therefore, you have to get and keep him aroused. Keep in mind that men are visual creatures and can be sexually aroused by sight alone. Since women aren't as visually inspired as men, that's often the part women tend to overlook. Everyone knows the right physical contact is needed, but you have to be equally attentive to what he sees and hears. These are all part of the responses or feedback you will be giving him while making love.

Most women think they are giving their man adequate feedback, but an adequate response isn't what you're going for. You need to give him something that he's never even imagined. After all, it's your husband—go for it. Here's what you need to do. I'll start with the visual first. Use your body to construct the most intense sexual image imaginable. If he kisses your neck, respond so he can see what he just did. If he touches a bikini spot—one of the areas normally covered by your bikini—throw your head back and run your fingers through your hair. When foreplay is over and he sends Willy in to work his wonders, you should orchestrate your body to paint an incredibly sensual picture in response to each bit of stimulus he gives you. Then other times, you want to make him think you've completely lost control of your body. It's all about making him see what he's doing to you. It will drive him crazy to see you squirm, arch, quiver, and shake. Many women can't truly put it on their man like they want because they get preoccupied with the thoughts of, *What will he think of me?* This is why you kept the piece in the first place. You're not worried about who he's going to tell or what your reputation will be in the morning. It's your husband, for God's sake. It's your job to know how to keep him.

The other critical piece of feedback he needs during intimacy is intense sexual, sensual, and sometimes uncontrollable sounds. Your sounds and the images you paint for him with your body should go hand in hand. When he does something stimulating, reward him with an unforgettable audible response. A man is always looking for your positive affirmations in bed. This is not the time to hold a conversation or to give a critique, though. You need to do those things well before you make your way to the bedroom. Your goal is to give him a positive and intense response each time he does something good.

Being great in bed involves a bit of theatrics. However, just like they do in Hollywood, you've got to make it believable. Most women go wrong by giving their man repetitious, predictable, and inhibited responses. When your husband notices that humdrum look on your face and sees that you're just going through the motions, trust me, it won't be long before he starts looking elsewhere for a little excitement.

Here are a few more ideas that will help to keep the fire in your love life. When you feel your man is settling into a sexual rut, flip the script. Do something you've never done. Consider these ideas:

1. Wear a wig.
2. Wear high heels and fishnet stockings while breaking him off some.
3. Change your bedtime clothing. If you wear lingerie often, come to bed with nothing on. If you normally wear nothing, try some lingerie. Dress up as someone he may have fantasies about (teacher, nurse, dominatrix, movie star, singer). You can really have fun with this one.
4. Buy him a pair of cheap, flimsy pajamas that you can literally rip off his body like a sex-starved lunatic.

5. Go to his office at lunchtime and break him off some.
6. Greet him at the door naked and ravage his body in the middle of the living room floor.
7. Surf the Web to find new positions you've never imagined.
8. Buy sex toys to explore different sensations.
9. If you're normally as quiet as a church mouse, howl like a hound dog. Vary your breathing.
10. Every now and then sacrifice "yours" so he can get "his." Give him a piece with complete disregard for yourself, even if that results in a sixty-second session.

This is your mate for life, so have fun with it. Marriage is the time when you want to bring down the house, but don't use up all your tricks in the first few months. Forever is a long time. Your husband may not have the desire for something different, but I suggest you put your creativity to work, just in case he gets a wild hair.

I know this may be a little awkward for a woman to hear coming from her father, but who would be better? If I'm asking you to keep the piece until you're married, I feel it's only right to give you the sexual knowledge you need when you don't have the experience to fall back on. I'd rather it be awkward than to allow you to learn from the streets. Enjoy your husband and the intimacy you share.

Your Partner in Crime

Creativity is also required outside of the bedroom. Just as you avoid the in-bed rut, you must make the same effort to avoid the out-of-bed one. All you need to do is make an effort. The people who allow themselves to get stuck in the marriage rut are the same ones who would be stuck in a rut if they were single. Again, the problem is not marriage, it's the individuals taking part in the marriage. Each person needs to commit to an active lifestyle early in the relationship and carry the practice over the years. If not, you'll be blaming marriage for your humdrum lifestyle too.

Have you ever noticed how boring and dull some married folks are? Look around, notice how they rarely smile, and barely look each other in the eye. This is a sign of laziness. These are the types of people who take each other for granted. There's a little game I like to play when I go out to eat that shows you how real this is. The next time you go to a restaurant, look around at the couples and watch their body language. Some couples are going to be staring dreamily into each other's eyes, others will be laughing hysterically, some will be engrossed in a deep conversation, and others will be snuggled up next to each other. On the other hand, pay attention to the couples who are not talking, not sitting near each other, and are showing absolutely no affection whatsoever. Without looking at their ring fingers, I try to pick out the ones who are married and those who aren't. I can always tell the ones who are married because they usually show the least amount of affection. I'm right 95 percent of the time. Don't let it happen to you.

Life is full of wonderful things to do, especially when you're married because that means you always have a companion. When you're single and want to play a game, you've got to find someone to play with you. If you want to go camping, to a movie, or to the mall, it's always more fun to go with a friend. Be thankful you don't have to do that. You've got a live-in friend, partner, and hangin' buddy. Don't wait for life to come to you; go out and get it. As long as you have each other, you've got all you need.

Set aside time to keep the life in your marriage. If you were single, you would probably make time to go dancing, to a movie, or to the park. Do the same thing when you're married. Plan yearly vacations. Go out for a drink. Set aside a weekly date night and continue to enjoy many of the things you did before you were married. Why wouldn't you when you always have each other? It's all what you make it.

TALK IS CHEAP

I don't believe marriage has to be riddled with drama and problems. Think about how often you've heard people say, "Marriage is tough," "Marriage is a full-time job," or "Marriage has its ups and downs." I believe if you go into marriage with the attitude that it's going to be a grind, that's exactly what it will be. A problem is only a problem when you view it as one. Attitude and communication are everything. You've got to be able to freely talk with your man, and you must build an environment where it is comfortable for him to talk freely to you as well. Open communication costs you absolutely nothing, but with it you can overcome just about any challenge you may face. When you come across what appears to be a problem, think of it as an opportunity to learn something you didn't know before. For example, you may look at algebra as a serious problem, but to an engineer it's a routine part of life. Crossing a river can be a huge problem, but not if you have a boat. Don't give energy to negativity. If you don't have the answer, talk to someone who has conquered the type of problem you're experiencing.

Open lines of communication are the best way to form an impenetrable bond between you and your husband. It is extremely important to know how to work through tough conversations without allowing the talks to push your relationship over the edge. In order for that to happen, you must develop a system to effectively communicate your feelings, concerns, and desires. Here are some quick and dirty guidelines that will keep you and your husband singing from the same sheet of music for years to come.

1. Always begin with a healthy dose of patience.

2. Talk slowly and methodically.

3. Learn to use *I* in your conversations more than *you*. Using the word *you* many times is interpreted as blaming and will cause him to shut down altogether. You can get the same point across by eliminating *you*.

4. Listen more than you talk.

5. When you do talk, do it for no more than a minute before giving him the opportunity to respond.

6. Periodically, after you've made an important point, ask him, "Does that make sense?" This question will go very far in bettering your communication with your man. Don't assume he understands. This will help to reduce the number of question marks floating around in your brain because you give him the opportunity to dive into more detail if he doesn't quite get it. If he gets it, then great. You've got confirmation that you were understood and your efforts weren't in vain. Try it. You'll be surprised as to how much it helps.

7. Once you've thoroughly listened to what he has to say, repeat it and ask confirming questions like, "Is that correct?" "Do I have that right?" Restating and

confirming is an incredibly helpful technique. It not only lets him know you were actually listening, but it gives him the opportunity to clarify if you didn't quite get his point. Don't move on to the next subject until he says, "Yes, you got that right."

8. After he has the opportunity to fully state his position, then state yours.

9. Finally, offer a solution. Men like solutions. The last thing you want to do is ramble on for hours about an issue and offer no advice for fixing it.

I know it sounds basic, but simple tips are often the most effective ones. You'd be surprised by the number of women who hurt their marriages merely by having poor communication practices. If you're disciplined about using these guidelines in the first few years of marriage, your husband will develop better communication skills by the example you set.

CHAPTER EIGHT

Power Reclaimed

DATING AND MARRIAGE DO NOT HAVE TO BE WAR. THEY CAN and should be the most wonderful experiences anyone could ever encounter. It's truly about setting standards for yourself and sticking to them. As a matter of fact, as I was writing this book, I discussed many of these subjects with friends and family, and they would tell me the type of woman I was describing in this book didn't exist, but I knew better. As fate would have it, I had the blessing of meeting and marrying the very woman who personifies all of the positive qualities of the woman I've described in this book. She's spiritual, fun-loving, smart, beautiful, streetwise, positive, family oriented, and has standards and values—a virtuous woman.

Men want women who have substance and character, but they're ultimately attracted to women who understand their worth. You have the answers in your hand. I stand behind this book to the point that I not only talked the talk, but I walked the walk by marrying a woman who understood her worth. I'm not saying she didn't make some of the very same mistakes I've described in this book before we met, but what I do know is that by the time I met her, she displayed a distinct intolerance for much of what she had dealt with from men in the past.

Trust me, marrying the right person is indeed worth the sacrifice of demanding a higher standard. It's not that hard. You owe it to yourself. Our children need fathers and mothers, not just baby mamas or baby daddies.

This book was intended to stir the pot a bit. I wanted to put a spotlight on women and their shortcomings in relationships, in hopes that it would be the spark to produce change. Yes, men absolutely have their issues as well—which I will thoroughly address in the near future—but if enough women are empowered to take the reins off their lives and not subject themselves to merely being a sexual play toy, men would be forced to adapt. Until this happens, the number of men not willing to commit to one woman and the ones who are socially irresponsible will continue to grow. Women must put their foot down to bring about change.

There were a number of men who told me I was saying too much. Those were also the men who were taking full advantage of a woman's vulnerability. I've been there myself. But men tend to change their tune when their daughters begin to come of age.

I hope you take this book and use it as a tool to promote discussion. Talk to your girlfriends. Discuss some of these subjects with the men in your life. Whatever you do, don't stop learning. The more you educate yourself, the better choices you'll make when selecting a man. Women are the true trendsetters in relationships. Don't just wish for dignity and respect, demand it. Too many women act as though they will never be able to get another man if they set the bar too high. That is so far from the truth. Men will always strive to attain the standard women put forth. If you expect the best, that's what you'll get. If you expect a man to be a scrub, that's what you'll get.

You will come across men who will disagree with some points I have made, and you will find many others who agree. The important thing is to always consider the source in addition to the person's MO. I personally feel there is nothing more important than marriage and family. Be careful taking the advice of men who subscribe to a less-than-honorable set of values.

Let me leave you with this: A woman is as precious as a diamond. It's only a stone, a natural part of the earth, right? But it's the most valuable stone on earth. Do you know why? It's because diamonds are purposely held off the market in order to dramatically limit their supply. That sends the value through the roof, making even the smallest piece greatly cherished. If you dramatically limit the piece you give out, you will be equally cherished too.

APPENDIX: PLAY YOUR CARDS RIGHT

We are all players in the relationship game of life. Whether you want to participate or not, you're in the game. Since you've got to play, you might as well understand the rules and strategies so you can be good at it. Like the game of poker, it's essential that you develop the art of bluffing or misleading someone into believing you can and will do something you're not capable of doing. Notice, I did not say lying. In poker, you usually try to bluff when your cards are not very good, but you attempt to mislead your opponent into thinking you have a great hand. In this day and age, men are bluffing women right out of their panties. But if you play your cards right while dating, a man doesn't have a choice but to honor the authority you hold as a woman.

By virtue of being a woman, you already hold the best cards in the deck—all four aces. There isn't a man out there who should be able to bluff you if you know you have a perpetual winning hand. Understanding the value of your cards is the secret to not being bluffed into giving away your most valuable ones. Every card you give away adds strength to the man's hand, so it's best to keep them all.

Let's take a look at your hand.

SELF: This ace of spades is your trump card. It can beat any other card in the deck. You must look at yourself in the mirror every day. Everything you do—your attitude, your perseverance, your dedication, and your respect for yourself—starts with you.

DATING: The ace of clubs. It's called a club for a reason. It's the big stick you carry to keep men in line. Dating is where you may run across all of the knuckleheads before you find that special one.

COMMITMENT: The ace of diamonds. This card represents the secrets to conducting yourself when you've found a special man. You should have made a mutual commitment, and if you've done what you're supposed to do, you might be receiving a diamond ring.

MARRIAGE: The ace of hearts. Your family is where your heart lies. This card holds the secrets to a long and joyful relationship with your husband.